THE NAKED TRUTH ABOUT TITHING AND GIVING TO THE CHURCH

THE NAKED TRUTH ABOUT TITHING AND GIVING TO THE CHURCH

JOHNNY L SHARP

All rights reserved under the U.S. copyright Act of 1976, no part of this publication may be reproduced, distributed, or transmitted in any form or by any means, or stored in a database or retrieval system, without the prior written permission of the publisher. If you would like to use this material from the book (other than review purposes), please contact the publisher at jsharplegacy@gmail.com.

Unless otherwise noted scriptures are taken from the THE HOLY BIBLE, NEW INTERNATIONAL VERSION® NIV®Copyright © 1973, 1978, 1984 by International Bible Society®Used by permission. All rights reserved worldwide.

Scripture noted KJV are taken from the New King James Version. Copyright © 1982 by Thomas Nelson, Inc. Used by Permission. All rights reserved.

Scripture noted AMP are quotations taken from the Amplified Bible, Copyright © 1954, 1958, 1962, 1964, 1965, 1987 by The Lockman Foundation. Used by Permission.

Scripture noted NKJV are taken from the New King James Version®. Copyright © 1982 by Thomas Nelson. Used by permission. All rights reserved.

ISBN-13: 9781978254336
ISBN-10: 1978254334
Library of Congress Control Number: 2017916398
CreateSpace Independent Publishing Platform
North Charleston, South Carolina

For booking arrangements, please contact Johnny Sharp at jsharplegacy@gmail.com. Visit me online at johnnysharp.com

DEDICATION

This book is dedicated to my late grandmother, Mary Sharp. My grandmother was an amazing woman, she exemplified humility, dedication and compassion to all those she encountered. My grandmother is accredited for instilling in me an internal belief that I was special and that I could accomplish anything I set my mind to do. I will eternally be grateful for her raising me to be the God-fearing man I am today.

To my Aunt Johnnie Mae, one of the most generous and caring people I know. During the time in my life God needed someone to step in and help me, you answered the call. I truly appreciate you for being an intricate part of my life.

To my amazing sisters, Ruby and Rochelle, thank you for a lifetime of love and support.

Last but certainly not least, to my two kids, Allison and Jon Sharp, you're the apples of my eye! You two are the most incredible kids in the entire world, I'm proud to be your dad!

ACKNOWLEDGEMENT

I would like to express my deepest gratitude to the many people who encouraged me to write and finish this book; to all those who provided support, talked things over, read, wrote, offered comments, allowed me to quote their remarks and assisted in the editing, proofreading and design. Thank you!

I would like to thank my God-father George Stewart for challenging me to publish this book. To my friend Renault Ross for motivating me during this project. I pray your book, "One Fry at a Time" continues to succeed!

I would like to thank Kay Allen for helping me in the process of selection, and proofreading this book.

Last and not least, I beg forgiveness of all those who have been with me over the course of this project and whose names I have failed to mention. Thank you for all your love and support!

REAL PEOPLE, REAL TESTIMONIES

This scripture-based Revelation gifted by Johnny Sharp solidified the True Freedom, True Peace & True Love that can only be found in an "Untainted" relationship with Jesus Christ! The guilt trip is over, the anxiety has ceased, and my heart is even more inspired to give from Love not out of obligation. Inspired by Truth, my life will never be the same!

K Allen

If you are ready to walk in freedom and no longer bound by the curse of not being able to give your 10% every payday according to Malachi 3:18," will a man rob God? Yes in tithes and offerings", then this book is for you. Johnny gives a detailed biblical study of tithing and he brings depth and clarity to the fact that Jesus nor his disciples taught on tithing. Be enlightened as I have been enlightened and give freely from your heart, no longer bound by the "curse" of the Law. You shall know the Naked Truth and it shall make you free!

D Maddox

I stopped tithing over 5 years ago. I use to be scared to go to church because I didn't have enough money. I remember this one time, I was going through such a financial struggle and all I had was change, so I said to myself, God knows what's happening, I'm sure he will be happy with whatever I can gfive, so I talked myself into going to service that day. When it came to the offering, I put all I had in the bucket only to be called out. Thank God, I wasn't called out by name, but the pastor got on the mic and said, "I know y'all not putting change in my baskets, some of y'all should be ashamed of yourself." My heart immediately dropped, I wanted to run and hide. A bunch of emotions ran through my mind, first I was hurt, then I became mad, very mad! I thought this place was a safe haven for people like me, just like the hospital for sick people. At this time, I was going through one of the hardest times in my life and instead of being uplifted and encouraged, I was shamed. I began to question if God was like this. Are their requirements for his love? Do I need to have all my stuff together first and then go to church? I say all this to say, after Johnny shared his book with me, it was a confirmation, a breath of fresh air! Finally, someone understood me! I was truly blessed to know that I was not alone. I hope this book blesses others as it has blessed me!

M Moore

TABLE OF CONTENTS

Dedication v

Acknowledgement vii

Real People, Real Testimonies viii

Preface Misconceptions of Tithing and Giving xiii

Chapter 1: What is the tithe and tithing? 1
  Part 1: What tithing is NOT 3
  Part 2: What is the tithe and tithing? 6
  Part 3: There were multiple types of tithe, not just one! 9

Chapter 2: The Purpose of tithing 12
  Part 1: The Laws of Moses – the Mosaic Law 14
  Part 2: The Argument: Tithing Origination 16
  Part 3: Pre-law: Abraham Tithe in Genesis - Part 1 18

Chapter 3: The Big Misconception- Malachi 3:8 · · · · · · · · · · · · · · · 30
  Part 1: Corruption in the Temple: Who's to blame? · · · · · · · · · · · · 36
  Part 2: The Storehouse is not the Church · · · · · · · · · · · · · · · · · · 42
  Part 3: Who's Really Robbing God? · 45

Chapter 4: Jesus on Tithing: Was it taught or commanded? · · · · · · 58
  Part 1: Did Jesus teach, command or endorse tithing in the
  New Testament? · 58
  Part 2: When did the Old Testament end and New Testament
  begin? · 62
  Part 3: Jesus' Perspective on Money. · 74

Chapter 5: Tithing in the New Testament · 83
  Part 1: Introduction: New Priesthood – New Law and Order · · · 83
  Part 2: The Book of Hebrews · 91
  Part 3: The Great Debate – Abraham's Tithe pt. 2 (Hebrews 7) · · · 94

Chapter 6: Apostle Paul on Tithing and Giving · · · · · · · · · · · · · · · 111
  Part 1: New Testament Giving · 111
  Part 2: Five Principles of New Testament Giving · · · · · · · · · · · · 139
  Part 3: The Prosperity Message · 164

Preface

MISCONCEPTIONS OF TITHING AND GIVING

Have you ever asked or heard someone ask one of these questions:

1. Are we obligated to tithe? Am I cursed if I don't tithe?
2. Is the tithe only money? Can I tithe my time or something else?
3. Is tithing the same as an offering or first-fruits?
4. My church teaches those that don't tithe are robbing God, is this true? Should I leave my church if they teach tithing?
5. Is it true tithing was under the law, therefore we shouldn't tithe since we're no longer under the law?

6. Did Jesus or any Apostle teach tithing?
7. Was tithing practiced in the New Testament?
8. Should I give to the church? Do I have to give only to the church? Can I give outside the church?
9. Why do churches always teach tithing from the Old Testament and not the New Testament?
10. Should we tithe because Abraham tithed?

In this book, we will explore the bible's many misconceptions of tithing and giving. My assignment is to correct the erroneous teachings pertaining to tithing and giving in today's church. We'll also address what is called pluralistic ignorance related to this erroneous teaching. Pluralistic ignorance is essentially a situation in which a majority of a group privately rejects a norm, but incorrectly assumes most others accept it, and therefore go along with it. This can also be described as, "No one believes, but everyone thinks that everyone believes." New Testament tithing is a prime example of pluralistic ignorance in today's church. Due to the fact no one can truly explain why New Testament Christians are required to tithe, most deep down inside reject the practice, yet accept it because most others accept it.

In preparing to write this book, I asked multiple people to share their understanding of why they tithe. I wasn't surprised to find most couldn't explain their reasoning, yet believed it was a requirement. Most believed it was a requirement because they were taught it was a requirement. However, admitted they often questioned it privately.

It has been my observation in the body of Christ we have a lot of churches with their own doctrines based off their own private interpretation of the bible. It has always baffled me that while we have the same God, same Jesus, same Holy Spirit, yet we have extreme differences when it comes to interpreting the same bible. It's frightening to say, but it's a fact, someone's private interpretation is wrong! I find most people are loyal to their church doctrine opposed to the pure unadulterated Word of God. Be mindful our commitment and loyalty should always be to the truth, not a church doctrine.

This message you're about to begin reading is going to test the very fiber of your commitment and loyalty to the truth. I'm curious how many will read and believe, yet reject, simply because it goes against their church doctrinal belief.

My assignment isn't to force you into believing, rather it's to provide you with The Naked Truth. The Naked Truth is intended to expose erroneous teachings that has been dressed as the truth and has been widely accepted as the truth. The Naked Truth about Tithing and Giving to the Church, is based upon this allegory.

THE ALLEGORY OF TRUTH AND LIE:

There were two individuals one named Truth and the other named Lie. They were hanging out at the lake, and Lie said to Truth, "I bet I can swim faster than you."

Truth replied, "I bet you can't."

Lie responded saying, "Then let's find out. You swim first and I'll time you."

Truth agreed, took off his clothes, and dives into the lake and began swimming. While he was swimming, Lie took off his clothes and put on his clothes. After he put his clothes on, he ran from the lake into the city. While he was running looking like Truth, people noticed and said, "Look at Truth running in the street."

Meanwhile Truth realized what Lie had done – he hurried out the lake and began pursuing Lie, naked. Those same people that saw Lie in Truth's clothes said, "Oh my goodness, look at Truth naked. There's the butt naked Truth!"

Once Truth finally caught up with Lie – he stripped him of his clothes, exposing him for the lie he was.

My assignment is to undress this erroneous teaching and share with you the real Truth. Thereafter, it's between you and God what you decide to do with it.

My Story:

Over the past twenty years, I've heard some of the best teachings on the subject of tithing and giving, taught by some of todays most respected teachers. Although some of those messages were taught well, meaning the **content** was truly bible-based, I've discovered the message, **context**, wasn't always biblically-based.

I grew up in a traditional church where tithing was never taught. At the tender age of eighteen I dedicated my life to Christ, thereafter I began consuming all the information I could find on serving Christ. I was hungry. Having spiritually outgrown my childhood church, I joined a non-denominational church that taught tithing as a requirement. Being new in the faith and desiring to be right with God, I embraced the teaching. After years of hearing tithing was a requirement from highly respected church leaders, I took tithing very seriously. Nevertheless, later in life I found being a consistent tither was more than a notion, paying ten percent was quite a challenge during life's financially challenging seasons. Quite frankly, I found myself many times unable to tithe. I can recall times it was either tithe or not pay an important financial obligation. I admit on some of those occasions I robbed God, at least that's what they called it when you don't tithe. Due to this, I lived much of my Christian life under a cloud of guilt and condemnation, believing God was angry with me. Maybe you can relate because the last I heard statistics indicate less than fifteen-percent of Christians tithe regularly. Based upon that statistic, we have a significant problem when eighty-five -percent of anything fails to participate. Either God isn't doing what he promised, "Opening up the Windows of Heaven and pouring us out a blessing we have no room to receive it", wherefore we have enough to both tithe and live, or perhaps we simply have a lot of Christians who are stealing God's money because they're greedy and thieves.

Teachers of tithing have very strong convictions when it comes to the message of tithing. This principle of tithing has become a *tenet* of most non-denominational church doctrines. It's taught with such conviction most members are even afraid to question the teaching. You're taught tithing is mandatory, especially for those who operate in some capacity of leadership, tithing is a prerequisite. Tithing is so critical to some churches that if you're a church member requesting financial assistance, oftentimes your giving record is reviewed for tithing. If it's discovered you're not a tither or an inconsistent tither, you could be easily denied assistance.

We can see this topic of tithing is no small matter to be ignored.

This *book will* give you a spiritual eye-opening revelation discovered on this subject. Due to the fact I personally had questions about tithing, I'm sure I'll address most yours.

Please understand this book is not designed to be just another good inspirational Christian book, rather a bible study. It's geared to educate you. I'm describing it as a study because God expects you to study and analyze the messages you receive.

2 Timothy 2:15 AMP says, "Study and be eager and do your utmost to present yourself to God approved (tested by trial), a workman who has no cause to be ashamed, correctly analyzing and accurately dividing (rightly handling and skillfully teaching) the Word of *Truth*."

This book is not intended to convince you over to my school of thought. No, it's going to provide you with chapters and verses to arrive at your own conclusion. Acts 17:11 says, " Now the Berean Jews were of more noble character than those in Thessalonica, **for they received the message with great eagerness and examined the Scriptures every day to see if what Paul said was true.**"

So don't take my word for it, God fully expects you and me to verify what we're being taught. One of the problems in today's church is most people don't want to study for themselves. It's easier to believe what you've heard without fact-checking. We are warned to be careful of what we hear and believe. Accepting whatever your leader teaches can be dangerous. We'll discuss that more in detail later in this book.

However, no one is above the written Word of God. Paul said in Galatians 1:8-9, "But even if we or an angel from heaven should preach a gospel other than the one we preached to you, let them be under God's curse! ⁹ As we have already said, so now I say again: If anybody is preaching to you a gospel other than what you accepted, let them be under God's curse!"

For Christians the bible should be our final source and authority. 2 Timothy 3:16 AMP says, "All Scripture is God-breathed [given by divine inspiration] and is profitable for instruction, for conviction [of sin], for correction [of error and restoration to obedience], for training in righteousness [learning to live in conformity to God's will, both publicly and privately—behaving honorably with personal integrity and moral courage]; so that the man of God may be complete *and* proficient, outfitted *and* thoroughly equipped for every good work."

Although you will learn tithing isn't a New Testament requirement, I want you to know that doesn't mean you're not expected to give, because you are. This book is NOT intended to stop or reduce your level of giving to your church. ***Again I repeat this book is not intended to stop or reduce your financial contributions to your church! Nor am I suggesting you leave your church if they teach tithing.*** My primary objective is to free you from any spiritual bondage related to the *mandatory* religious practice of tithing. Hereafter, whether you continue to tithe or not won't send you to hell. God loves you regardless.

> *"The theme of this book is about knowing the truth and being set-free!"*

Religion is composed of man's requirements to please God. That's why there are so many religions in our society today because of man and our different philosophies. Some religions paint an ugly picture of God being like an angry landlord on the first of the month demanding his tithe in full, and if you don't have it, he mercilessly kicks you out on the streets. I've discovered this isn't the God of the New Testament. God isn't demanding the tithe because love doesn't force people's compliance. We're no longer under the old covenant of laws that requires performance, we're under a new covenant of grace that requires us to simply receive. Ephesians 2:8-9 NKJV says, "For it is by grace you have been saved, through faith—and this is not from yourselves, it is the gift of God—not by works, so that no one can boast.."

It's not God that has put people into bondage with all these religious rules, it is man. Paul experienced this same issue during his time when some attempted to demand Titus to be circumcised. Paul states in Galatians 2:3-6, "Yet not even Titus, who was with me, was compelled to be circumcised, even though he was a Greek. This matter arose *because some false believers* had infiltrated our ranks to spy on the freedom we have in Christ Jesus and to make us slaves. We did not give in to them for a moment, so that the truth of the gospel might be preserved for you. As for those who were held in high esteem—whatever they were makes no difference to me; God does not show favoritism—they added nothing to my message.

To appreciate this you must first understand circumcision was a practice of the Old Testament. That practice among others were no longer valid to Christianity in the New Testament era. However Paul indicates, there were some, he described as "false believers" who sought opportunity to demand they re-conform to those old outdated practices. Paul said NO!

My question for you is, "What erroneous teachings taught by man (false brethren) have you accepted that keeps you in *religious* bondage?" Be mindful, God doesn't have you in this religious bondage, you've allowed a man to place you there. After reading this book you will be enabled to be bold like Paul and stand flat-footed and say no to tithing and other Old Testament practices and requirements that hold you in bondage.

This book is intended to show you that while tithing is not a requirement, God does expect us to give in the New Testament, and he has prescribed a way for us to do it.

For this study, I encourage you to follow these tips:

1) Use your bible to follow along and verify each scripture reference.
2) Read thoroughly, refrain from skipping ahead.
3) If necessary, ask questions. I'm an email away.
4) Desire to know the truth despite what you've been taught.
5) Lastly, love God more than you love your church doctrine.

My prayer for you:

That the God of our Lord Jesus Christ, the Father of glory, may give unto you the spirit of wisdom and revelation in the knowledge of him. That the eyes of your understanding be enlightened that you may know the hope of his calling and the exceeding greatness of his power toward us who believe, according to the working of his mighty power. I pray that you know the truth and that truth make you free - in Jesus name.

Amen!

Chapter 1

WHAT IS THE TITHE AND TITHING?

When I began writing this book, I asked numerous people and posed this question, *"What is the tithe and tithing?"* The common answer I received was the tithe is giving ten-percent of one's income to their church. It is true the tithe by definition does mean a tenth, I don't think anyone will argue that fact. However, people very rarely get hung-up on the definition of *the tithe*, rather it's the *understanding of tithing* where the true problem stems.

So what is tithing? Tithing can be simply understood as the act of presenting the tithe.

There are many opinions regarding the act of tithing. It generally varies from church to church and from individual to individual. If you were to ask five individuals, "What is the act of tithing," you'll likely get five different responses.

Some will say,

1) "It's giving 10% of your *gross* paycheck to their church."
2) "It's giving 10% of your *net* income."
3) "It's giving 10% to people in need – charitable donations."
4) "It's not all money, rather it can be 10% of your time as well."
5) "It's giving 10% of ALL the money you get, including money that is borrowed."

> *"People rarely misunderstand the tithe, rather the act of tithing."*

Considering people have so many misconceptions regarding the act of tithing, it's necessary that we take a comprehensive look at what tithing *is* and more importantly what tithing is *not*.

PART 1: WHAT TITHING IS NOT

Deuteronomy 12:6 – *There you shall take your [1]burnt offerings, your [2]sacrifices, your [3]tithes, the [4]heave offerings of your hand, your [5]vowed offerings, your [6]freewill offerings, and the [7]firstborn of your herds and flocks.*

Notice here in this verse, it listed tithes among the various types of ceremonial offerings. As you see there were multiple types of offerings: burnt offering, sacrifices, heave offering, vowed offering, freewill offering and the firstborn of the herds and flocks. Tithes are mutually exclusive to these offerings, meaning they are not the same.

It's important for us to dispel the belief that tithing is the same as giving a freewill offering or of giving the first which is referred to as "firstling," notably regarded as the firstborn and firstfruits.

We can clearly see tithing was not the same as giving the firstlings. Remember the firstlings are the firstborn and firstfruits. Here's a practical way of differentiating the difference between these two terms. We can say the **tithes** is a "tenth of," whereas the **firstlings** which is the firstborn and firstfruits are the "first of."

Principle of the firstlings:

a. **Firstborn**: has to do with God commanding the first-born sons and/or beast to be dedicated to him. Reference: [Ex. 13:2; Num. 3:13; Num. 18:15-17]

b. **Firstfruits**: has to do with God commanding the first-fruits of our agricultural produce harvest. Reference: [Ex. 23:19 & 34:19; Lev. 2:14]

I want to debunk the false ideal that the tithe and firstfruits are synonymous. Many people inappropriately use these terms tithe and firstfruits interchangeably. That is not correct, they are totally different. It's imperative to understand that the firstfruit is not the same as the tithe, because those that teach tithing sometimes suggest tithers are to give the "first of" their increase/income to God. I believe this is why there's great confusion centered on whether people should tithe from their net income or their gross income. Some churches teach tithes should come from ALL of one's gross income (increase). Gross income is what you make BEFORE deductions, whereas net income is what you make AFTER deductions. This erroneous belief the tithe should come from the gross is derived from the misinterpretation of Proverbs 3:9-10.

Question: During the church collection of the "tithe" and offering. Have you ever heard this commonly stated? **"Honor the Lord with your possessions, and with *the 'firstfruits' of all your increase*;** so your barns will be filled with plenty, and your vats will overflow with new wine." Proverbs 3:9-10

It's obvious this verse is about firstfruits, it clearly states it, however many preachers imply it's about tithing.

As a result of people using firstfruits and tithing interchangeably, many believers are discombobulated on whether to tithe off their net income or their gross income. This confusion stem from this passage being commonly misconstrued - taken out of context. It's been often taught to apply to the act of tithing, however in its proper context, it would only apply to giving the firstfruit offerings, not tithes.

Note: Based upon the logic we should tithe today. If we're required to tithe in the New Testament then we're also obligated to give firstfruits offerings off ALL our increase.

"The tithe is not synonymous to the firstfruits."

Important fact: Firstfruits was the first of *only* agricultural produce. Whereas the tithe was a tenth of *both* agricultural produce and livestock.

In the light of that understanding, it should be easy to understand this passage. God is saying if they were to give the firstfruits of the increase -harvest (agricultural produce), he would fill their barns with plenty (agricultural produce) – not money! Now you can see why it states your *barns will be filled*. What do farmers mainly put inside barns – agricultural produce, right? The promise was if you sow your firstfruits (agricultural produce), you will reap a substantial harvest. I can't emphasize it enough how important it is to understand bible context so these principles and others don't get intermingled.

Note: Bible scholars may suggest this verse is about agricultural produce only because they didn't have money in circulation during this period of time; wherefore God requested agricultural produce only because they didn't have money. That's false! Money was absolutely in circulation during this period of time. I will prove this fact in Part 2 - What is the tithe and tithing.

I want you to remember, **"Tithing is a "Percentage of" not the "First of"**. In God's instructions on tithing, he never required it to be the "First of".

PART 2: WHAT IS THE TITHE AND TITHING?

I. AS WE DISCUSSED EARLIER, THE TITHE MEANS A TENTH.

Leviticus 27:32 NKJV– *And concerning the tithe of the herd or the flock, of whatever passes under the rod, the **tenth one** shall be holy to the Lord.*

Notice this verse clearly proves our point, that the tithe isn't the first of rather the tenth of.

II. THE TITHE WAS A HOLY THING.

Leviticus 27:30 NKJV - *A tithe of everything from the land, whether grain from the soil or fruit from the trees, belongs to the Lord;* **it is holy to the Lord.**

In the Old Testament because the tithe was considered holy to the Lord, withholding the tithe produced a curse whereas obedience resulted in blessings.

III. TITHING WAS PRIMARILY AGRICULTURAL PRODUCE AND LIVESTOCK, NOT *MONEY*.

Leviticus 27:30-32 says, "A **tithe** of everything from the land, whether grain from the soil or fruit from the trees, belongs to the Lord; it is holy to the Lord. Whoever would redeem any of their tithe must add a fifth of the value to it. Every **tithe** of the herd and flock—every tenth animal that passes under the shepherd's rod—will be holy to the Lord.

Deuteronomy 14:22 - *Be sure to set aside a tenth of all that your **fields produce** each year.*

Tithing was mainly agricultural produce and livestock, not money. In case you're wondering if money was even in circulation during this period of time – it was. However, money was only used under certain circumstances for tithing.

Deuteronomy 14:22-26 says, "Be sure to set aside a tenth of all that your fields produce each year. Eat the tithe of your grain, new wine and olive oil, and the firstborn of your herds and flocks in the presence of the Lord your God at the place he will choose as a dwelling for his Name, so that you may learn to revere the Lord your God always. But if that place is too distant and you have been blessed by the Lord your God and cannot carry your tithe (because the place where the Lord will choose to put his Name is so far away), then exchange your tithe for **silver**, and take the **silver** with you and go to the place the Lord your God will choose. Use the **silver** to buy whatever you like: cattle, sheep, wine or other fermented drink, or anything you wish. Then you and your household shall eat there in the presence of the Lord your God and rejoice.

Silver was money. So this passage proves money was in circulation during this period of time. Nevertheless, we find it was only used as the exception for tithing, rather than the rule. Deuteronomy 14:25-26 clearly explains this exception. I've heard those who advocate tithing say the reason why they tithed agricultural produce and livestock in the Old Testament tithing system was because there wasn't any money in circulation during the time. We can clearly see that money did exist, therefore that statement isn't true.

PART 3: THERE WERE MULTIPLE TYPES OF TITHE, NOT JUST ONE!

Question: Did you know there were multiple types of tithes in the Old Testament? If you were like me, your answer would be no; but yes there were multiple types of tithes described in the Old Testament, specifically three. It's crucial we know this important fact regarding the Old Testament tithing system, because tithing teachers today focus only on one. They glean from these Old Testament tithing principles, yet they fail to fully understand tithings multi-facet applications.

The "3" types of tithes:

1) The Levitical tithe [Num. 18:21-29; Neh.10:37-38]

    The Levitical tithe – was a required tithe from the nation of Israel to give on a yearly basis. They were required to give a tenth of everything in their land, herds, and flocks. The Levitical priest in turn were required to give a tenth of the best part of the tithe to the Aaronic priests.

2) The Festival tithe [Deut. 12: 5-7; Deut. 14: 22 -26]

    The Festival tithe - was another yearly required tithe. This tithe was brought to Jerusalem, where everybody celebrated before the Lord as they ate their portions of this tithe.

3) The Poor tithe [Deut. 14: 28, 29 ; 26: 12]

The Poor tithe – was a triennial required tithe. Triennial, meaning they were required to give this tithe once every three years. This tithe was required to be stored where the poor could come and eat and be satisfied.

Most teachers, who teach tithing is for the New Testament, fail to explain these different types of tithes and application thereof. If I were to question why, they'd likely say, "We don't follow the post-law practice of tithing rather the pre-law practice of tithing – referring to Abraham." Well if that's the case, they MUST refrain from using anything pertaining to tithing from Moses instituting the Law in Exodus, until the time Jesus died; considering everything between this period of time was considered the post-law (Mosaic Law) form of tithing. Therefore, in light of this insight, Malachi 3:8 "Will a man rob God" is no longer applicable when teaching tithing since it was under the Mosaic Law.

Following the completion of this chapter you should have a grasp on what tithing **is** as well as what tithing is **not**. This chapter focused on the *post-law* side of tithing, referring to the time when and after the Law of Moses was instituted in Exodus. Whereas the *Pre-law* pertains to the book of Genesis before the Law of Moses was instituted. So why did we began with the Post-law side of tithing? *Simply because the post-law form of tithing under the Law of Moses, the Mosaic Law, is the only place you can find God both prescribe "command" and describe "give instructions" on tithing.* Even though we observe another case of tithing in Genesis, you won't find it directly commanded by God.

This account of tithing is considered *Pre-law*, because it was done before the Law of Moses. We will address this pre-law account of tithing as seen in Genesis in our next chapter.

Term meanings:

* **Post- law:** After the Law of Moses was instituted - Effective: From Moses returning from Mt. Sinai with the Law until Jesus' death.
* **Pre-law:** Before the Law of Moses was instituted - The Book of Genesis only.

Chapter 2

THE PURPOSE OF TITHING

When purpose is not known, abuse is inevitable – Miles Monroe

The Purpose

I know you were astonished with some of the information regarding tithing shared in Chapter 1 of our study. You may have found there was a thing or two you didn't know about tithing. Now in this Chapter, we're going to examine the purpose of the tithe. As I stated before, *people very rarely get hung-up on the definition of the tithe, rather they misunderstand the act of tithing.*

In Chapter 2, I want to examine the purpose of the tithe. This part is crucial to understand, because when purpose is unknown or misunderstood, abuse or improper use is inevitable. Due to our lack of understanding related to tithing in today's church, tithing is being improperly used to require people to give.

So how do we determine the purpose? Whenever you attempt to determine the purpose of a thing you must consult the maker. In this case, the maker is God. God gave Moses the law on Mount Sinai to share with the nation of Israel [Ex. 31:18]. This law was referred to as the Law of Moses, also known as, the Mosaic Law. The institution of the Mosaic Law was a God ideal, not a man's good ideal. Therefore it's only right we seek God's Word to understand his original intentions for instituting this law.

The law was instituted after the children of Israel left Egypt and came to Mount Sinai, the Lord gave Moses the laws by which the people of Israel were to abide [Ex. 20:1-17]. Among the laws were the rules for the Levitical priesthood, its ritual service of the tabernacle, and the rituals and schedule of blood sacrifices and offerings [Lev. 1:1-2]. This law was only intended to be temporary until Jesus carried out his purpose in fulfilling it. In Matthew 5:17, Jesus says, "Do not think that I came to destroy the Law or the Prophets. I did not come to destroy but to fulfill."

Important fact: Whenever God commands something to be done, he always give instructions how he wants it done, he leaves no room for the opinion of man. Remember this bible principle what God prescribes "commands", he also describes "provide instructions."

So let's examine Gods purpose for the tithe under the Mosaic Law.

PART 1: THE LAWS OF MOSES – THE MOSAIC LAW

The Mosaic Law was given specifically to the nation of Israel. [Ex. 19; Lev. 26:46; Rom. 9:4]. The Law was composed of three parts: The Ten Commandments, the Ordinances and the Worship System which included the priesthood, the tabernacle, the offerings, and the festival. [Ex. 20-40; Lev. 1-7; 23]

The Mosaic Law came on the heels of the children of Israel's supernatural deliverance out of Pharaoh's bondage. Tithing was one of many systems commanded by God under this law, however for the interest of our study we will examine the purpose of the tithe under this Law.

As we discussed in Chapter 1, there were (3) different types of tithe and applications thereof. There was the Levitical tithe, the Festival tithe and the Poor tithe. While all these tithes were imperative, the Levitical tithe epitomizes the underlining purpose of the tithe some practice today.

The primary purpose of the tithe was for the Levitical Priesthood. According to Numbers 3:1-12 the Levite Priest were the sons of Aaron, divinely selected by God to attend to the needs of the children of Israel in things pertaining to the tabernacle.

Important fact: All priest had to be Levites, however all Levites were not priest.

Hezekiah assigned the priests and Levites to divisions—each of them according to their duties as priests or Levites—to offer burnt offerings and fellowship offerings, to minister, to give thanks and to sing praises at the gates of the Lord's dwelling. The king contributed from his own possessions for the morning and evening burnt offerings and for the burnt offerings on the Sabbaths, at the New Moons and at the appointed festivals as written in the Law of the Lord. **He ordered the people living in Jerusalem to give the portion due the priests and Levites so they could devote themselves to the Law of the Lord.** As soon as the order went out, the Israelites generously gave the firstfruits of their grain, new wine, olive oil and honey and all that the fields produced. They brought a great amount, a tithe of everything. The people of Israel and Judah who lived in the towns of Judah also brought a tithe of their herds and flocks and a tithe of the holy things dedicated to the Lord their God, and they piled them in heaps. [2 Chronicles 31:2-6]

The Lord said to Aaron, "You will have no inheritance in their land, nor will you have any share among them; I am your share and your inheritance among the Israelites. **"I give to the Levites all the tithes in Israel as their**

inheritance in return for the work they do while serving at the tent of meeting. [Numbers 18:20-21]

Some of today's teachers who teach tithing base their teachings on the Levitical tithing principle. They teach as the Levite Priest were God's representatives and they were required to receive the tithe, a tenth of, from the people. We are likewise required to give a tenth of our income to our local churches. There are many flaws to that comparison. However, the biggest one is the church only focuses on INCOME, whereas the Levitical tithe focused primarily on agricultural produce and livestock - not money. As we learned in Part One, money was only used as the exception, not the rule. See [Deut. 14: 22-26] for a reference.

In my conclusion of the purpose of the tithe, it was my objective to show you God's intentions for instituting the tithe under the Mosaic Law. God does everything on purpose for a purpose. When He commands something, he will leave no latitude for speculation or the opinions of man. We can safely dismiss the belief that the Levitical tithe is applicable to today's church.

PART 2: THE ARGUMENT: TITHING ORIGINATION

I'm calling this point, The Argument, because many opponents of tithing attempt to substantiate their belief based upon this reasoning. Opponents of tithing argue, "Since tithing originated under the Old Testament Mosaic Law, and we're no longer under the Old Testament law, we're exempt from tithing today." Opponents of the doctrine of tithing have used this argument for years in an attempt to debunk the practice of New Testament practice of tithing.

So let me address the question, did tithing originate under the Old Testament Mosaic Law? The answer is No, it didn't originate under the law however it *was* commanded under the Mosaic Law, not before. Read this again slowly so you can really comprehend, tithing did not originate under the Mosaic Law, however it wasn't required **until** the Mosaic Law was instituted.

Easy way to understand this concept:

* Tithing before the Mosaic Law – Voluntary
* Tithing after the Mosaic Law – Involuntary
* Tithing in the New Testament – Not Required

In Genesis we will find that Abraham did tithe once. The period of time between Abraham tithe and the actual law being instituted would be over 430 years' later.

Galatians 3:16-17 says, "The promises were spoken to Abraham and to his seed. Scripture does not say "and to seeds," meaning many people, but "and to your seed," meaning one person, who is Christ. What I mean is this:

The law, introduced 430 years later, does not set aside the covenant previously established by God and thus do away with the promise."

As you can see, the law came four-hundred and thirty years after Abraham. Proponents who teach tithing absolutely delight in disproving this argument. Commonly those that teach tithing point to Abrahams' tithing account in Genesis as the pre-law tithing example we should follow in the New Testament. While I agree with some teachings, that tithing did not originate under the law, I believe there is one major discrepancy in their belief system. Nowhere in Genesis do we find a <u>*command* to tithe, compared to Gods direct *command* to tithe under the Mosaic Law</u>.

PART 3: PRE-LAW: ABRAHAM TITHE IN GENESIS - PART 1

In Genesis, God *never* commanded Abraham or Jacob to tithe therefore we cannot assume it was a requirement. We can only speculate and theorize, however we CANNOT be (matter-of-fact) on this issue. Some theologians believe Abrahams' tithe was culturally influenced. Whether that's true or not, I won't leave it to conjecture to make that a fact. I will remain silent on matters God didn't distinctly make known, apparently it wasn't critical or else we wouldn't have to theorize. In the court of law if you cannot prove a major component of your case – your case is lost. I believe this simple observation annuls their case, that Abrahams' tithe was a requirement.

Once again, I say this because there are *no commands from God* to tithe, or any demonstration of anyone else tithing beside Abraham in Genesis, although some debate that Jacob did tithe as well. We will examine Jacob's account, and I will show you that Jacob's offering was not an act of tithing.

ABRAHAM TITHE

When Abram heard that his relative had been taken captive, he called out the 318 trained men born in his household and went in pursuit as far as Dan. During the night Abram divided his men to attack them and he routed them, pursuing them as far as Hobah, north of Damascus. He recovered all the goods and brought back his relative Lot and his possessions, together with the women and the other people. After Abram returned from defeating Kedorlaomer and the kings allied with him, the king of Sodom came out to meet him in the Valley of Shaveh (that is, the King's Valley). Then Melchizedek king of Salem brought out bread and wine. He was priest of God Most High, and he blessed Abram, saying, "Blessed be Abram by God Most High, Creator of heaven and earth. And praise be to God Most High, who delivered your enemies into your hand." Then Abram gave him a tenth of everything.

The king of Sodom said to Abram, "Give me the people and keep the goods for yourself. But Abram said to the king of Sodom, "With raised hand I have sworn an oath to the LORD, God Most High, Creator of heaven and earth,that I will accept nothing belonging to you, not even a thread or the strap of a sandal, so that you will never be able to say, 'I made Abram rich. I will accept nothing but what my men have eaten and the share that belongs to the men who went with me—to Aner, Eshkol and Mamre. Let them have their share." [Genesis 14:14-24]

This passage *describes* Abraham tithing to Melchizedek King of Salem and high priest of the Most High God. This passage is what teachers of tithing use to substantiate their New Testament tithing doctrine. Their premise is, "If Abraham was our example and he tithed *before* the Mosaic Law, we should continue to tithe today."

So let's delve into this passage and determine if this doctrine *fits* and comes perfectly together like a puzzle. The late attorney Johnnie Cochran is best remembered for his famous closing statement in the O J Simpson case, "If it don't fit, you must acquit." That is true for the Word of God, it should never contradict itself. If it doesn't fit, that indicates something isn't correct.

Some believe if Abraham tithed before the Mosaic Law, we should follow his example and tithe today. This is the basis of most non-denominational church tithing doctrine.

Observation 1: Genesis 14 account of Abraham tithing to Melchizedek is the *only* reference that *describes* him tithing. God's principle in mandating something has always been, "What he prescribes, **commands**, he describes, **provides instructions**." Basically if he, God, intended for Abraham to be our example of tithing he would have not only commanded it, he also would have provided instructions as well.

In Genesis 17 it depicts a perfect example of this principle. God prescribes, commands, Abraham on circumcision; then he describes, instructs, him on how it should be administered.

Genesis 17:9-14, "Then God said to Abraham, "As for you, you must keep my covenant, you and your descendants after you for the generations to come. This is my covenant with you and your descendants after you, the covenant you are to keep: <u>Every male among you shall be circumcised. You are to undergo circumcision, and it will be the sign of the covenant between me and you</u>. **(The command – God prescribing)**

<u>For the generations to come every male among you who is eight days old must be circumcised, including those born in your household or bought with money from a foreigner—those who are not your offspring. Whether born in your household or bought with your money, they must be circumcised. My covenant in your flesh is to be an</u>

<u>everlasting covenant. Any uncircumcised male, who has not been circumcised in the flesh, will be cut off from his people; he has broken my covenant</u>." **(Provide instructions – God describing)**

Observation 2: God only commanded us in the New Testament to follow Abraham's example of faith.

Romans 4:1-12 says, "What then shall we say that Abraham, our forefather according to the flesh, discovered in this matter? If, in fact, Abraham was justified by works, he had something to boast about—but not before God. What does Scripture say? "Abraham believed God, and it was credited to him as righteousness." Now to the one who works, wages are not credited as a gift but as an obligation. However, to the one who does not work but trusts God who justifies the ungodly, their faith is credited as righteousness. David says the same thing when he speaks of the blessedness of the one to whom God credits righteousness apart from works: "Blessed are those whose transgressions are forgiven, whose sins are covered. Blessed is the one whose sin the Lord will never count against them." Is this blessedness only for the circumcised, or also for the uncircumcised? We have been saying that Abraham's faith was credited to him as righteousness. Under what circumstances was it credited? Was it after he was circumcised, or before? It was not after, but before! And he received circumcision as a sign, a seal of the righteousness that he had by faith while he was still uncircumcised. So then, he is the father of all who believe but have not been circumcised, in order that righteousness might be credited to them. **And he is then also the father of the circumcised who not only are circumcised but <u>who also follow in the footsteps of the faith that our father Abraham</u> had before he was circumcised.**

Abraham tithe was not an act of faith. It was an act of gratitude and appreciation in *response* to the blessing he'd receive from Melchizedek. Then Melchizedek king of Salem brought out bread and wine. He was priest of God Most High, and he blessed Abram, saying, "Blessed be Abram by God Most High, Creator of heaven and earth. And praise be to God Most High, who delivered your enemies into your hand." **Then Abram gave him a tenth of everything.** [Genesis 14:18–20]

There is no evidence Abrahams' tithe was mandatory. Apart from seeing a direct command from God, we must surmise it was a voluntary act that perhaps may have been influenced by the customs of that time.

Observation 3: Abraham not only gave the tithe "a tenth" of his spoil away, He gave it *all* away!

We know Abraham gave a tenth of his spoil to Melchizedek, but did you know he gave the rest away as well? Abraham gave the rest of the spoil to the King of Sodom, with the exception of the portion his soldiers ate.

Genesis 14:20-24 says, "[20]And praise be to God Most High, who delivered your enemies into your hand." Then Abram gave him a tenth of everything. [21] The king of Sodom said to Abram, "Give me the people and keep the goods for yourself." [22] But Abram said to the king of Sodom, **"With raised hand I have sworn an oath to the Lord, God Most High, Creator of heaven and earth, [23] that I will accept nothing** belonging to you, not even a thread or the strap of a sandal, so that you will never be able to say, 'I made Abram rich.' [24] I will accept nothing but what my men have eaten and the share that belongs to the men who went with me—to Aner, Eshkol and Mamre. Let them have their share."

This passage further supports the fact Abraham tithe and offering was completely voluntary. Abraham advised the king in verse 21 that he made an oath to God not to keep anything. He stated, "Give me the people and keep the goods for yourself." Abram said to the king of Sodom, "With raised hand I have sworn an oath to the Lord, God Most High, Creator of heaven and earth, that I will accept nothing belonging to you, not even a thread or the strap of a sandal, so that you will never be able to say, I made Abram rich."

The overall point is he gave it **all** away, not just the tithe – the tenth. I'm also fully aware these goods he gave away initially belonged to the King of Sodom. However, when the King of Sodom lost the battle, he lost his goods. That is how it worked, the winner took all. Wherefore, when Abraham won the battle, the goods rightfully belonged to him. So technically if we are to follow Abraham's precise example we cannot omit this part. We would have to give ALL our money away, not just the tenth. Why aren't we following this example of Abraham giving? Are we cherry-picking our Abrahamic practices? That would beg to question, does God expect us to give all our income away? That would be absurd wouldn't it? There's absolutely no evidence that God expects us to give all our income away.

Genesis 13:2 - And Abram was very rich in cattle, in silver, and in gold.

If Abraham practiced giving all his money away, he wouldn't have been rich. Abraham was loaded, therefore when he received this spoil "wind-fall income", he was in a strong financial position many aren't in, to give it all away.

We'll discuss later Abraham receiving money and livestock from a king Genesis 20:10-16, but didn't tithe. Question: If tithing was a requirement, why wouldn't he tithe again? This entire account in Genesis 14 of Abraham tithing speaks to him following his heart in giving. There were no direct orders from God to give either one of these Kings anything – the tithe or offering. Both gifts were simply voluntary acts from his heart.

JACOBS' ALLEGED TITHE

In Genesis Chapter 28, we find an instance of what some teachers of tithing suggest demonstrate another example of pre-law tithing. After studying this, I categorically disagreed with that perspective, this was not an act of tithing either.

Genesis 28:12-22 says, "[12] He had a dream in which he saw a stairway resting on the earth, with its top reaching to heaven, and the angels of God were ascending and descending on it. [13] There above it stood the Lord, and he said: "I am the Lord, the God of your father Abraham and the God of Isaac. I will give you and your descendants the land on which you are lying. [14] Your descendants will be like the dust of the earth, and you will spread out to the west and to the east, to the north and to the south. All peoples on earth will be blessed through you and your offspring. [15] I am with you and will watch over you wherever you go, and I will bring you back to this land. I will not leave you until I have done what I have promised you." ¹⁶ When Jacob awoke from his sleep, he thought, "Surely the Lord is in this place, and I was not aware of it." ¹⁷ He was afraid and said, "How awesome is this place! This is none other than the house of God; this is the gate of heaven." ¹⁸ Early the next morning Jacob took the stone he had placed under his head and set it up as a pillar and poured oil on top of it. ¹⁹ He called that place Bethel, though the city used to be called Luz. ²⁰ <u>Then Jacob made a **vow**, saying, **"If** God will be with me and will watch over me on this journey I am taking and will give me food to eat and clothes to wear</u> ²¹so that I return safely to my father's household, then the Lord will be my God ²²and this stone that I have set up as a pillar will be God's house, and of all that you give me <u>I will give you a tenth</u>."

Observation 1: Verse 20 tells us clearly what Jacob did. Jacob made a *vow* to God.

There is no need for interpretation its right there in front of us, in verse 20. Jacob made a **vow** to God, a vow is a contingency offer to God. However, if and when God does his part, you're liable to fulfill your promise made. In this time these types of vows were not uncommon. When people were in unique situations and desperately needed God's supernatural favor, they made vows to evoke God's help.

1 Samuel 1:11 - And she **vowed a vow**, and said, O LORD of hosts, **if** thou wilt indeed look on the affliction of thine handmaid, and remember me, and not forget thine handmaid, but wilt give unto thine handmaid a man child, then I will give him unto the LORD all the days of his life, and there shall no razor come upon his head.

Observation 2: This could not be a demonstration of tithing

Tithing isn't optional, it's a requirement. Jacob said he would give a tenth *if* his request was honored. That statement doesn't fit the definition of tithing, however, it does fit the definition of making a vow. Vows were optional, whereas tithing wasn't. I want to also point out he didn't call it a tithe. The art of making a vow to God was sort of like negotiating a business deal. You want the deal to be mutually beneficial – a win-win situation. In the light of understanding that, how could Jacob make giving the tenth appealing if it belonged to God anyway? Think about it.

Despite Jacob's act not being an act of tithing, we can plainly see both his and Abraham's experiences were completely voluntary acts. If it was so critical for us to follow these examples as some suggest, we wouldn't have to infer so much from these two scenarios. In a period of four-hundred-thirty-years if tithing was a mandatory pre-law practice, we would see far more evidence of this being a common practice.

More on the Abraham tithe in chapter 5…

Chapter 3

THE BIG MISCONCEPTION - MALACHI 3:8

Introduction: Malachi the Big Misconception

In this part we will begin to delve into the heart of the misconception of the tithing doctrine. The third chapter of Malachi has been the premiere chapter used to provoke Christians to tithe. Most church leaders that promote New Testament tithing use this chapter as the basis to support their doctrine (body or system of teachings relating to a particular subject).

Take a moment and think about the last teaching you heard on tithing, or the last time you heard tithing being encouraged during the offering. Maybe not every time, but most of the time I'm sure you've heard the phrase, "Will a man rob God," mentioned. The implication is if you don't tithe you're stealing Gods money.

Malachi 3:*8 - Will a man rob God? Yet ye have robbed me. But ye say, wherein have we robbed thee? In tithes and offerings.*

As you can see a great deal of the tithing message derived from Malachi chapter 3 is largely responsible for invoking fear into the hearts of many believers, including myself at one given time. The message in a nut shell implies if we tithe we're blessed. However if we don't, we're robbing God and we live under a curse. This message is why I struggled with guilt and condemnation for my tithing inconsistency.

Christians who struggle to tithe are described as robbers and thieves for "stealing" God's money, with such strong language, who wouldn't feel condemned?

The undertone of this message is rooted in fear and has placed many Christians into spiritual bondage. This fear runs deep! In fact, most Christians are even afraid to question or challenge the practice of tithing in the New Testament, as I'm doing. I know for certain, based upon the conversations I've had with people from the past and present, most of them admit they've always questioned why the practice of tithing wasn't taught or demonstrated by any of the Apostles in the New Testament.

Given the vast misconception of Malachi, I decided to provide an entire chapter discussing this Old Testament book. In this part of our study, I intend to show you that Malachi 3:8 has been grossly misconstrued. What you will learn about this book is going to be shocking and a game-changer. I assure you once you finish this this part of our study, you will know who the true, "God Robber" was and presently is today.

Here are the points I intend showing you:

1) Malachi 3:8 message was not directed to the people, rather the priest.
2) This system of tithing and offerings was under the Mosaic Law.
3) This message in principle and practice was NOT intended to be practiced by New Testament believers.
4) In the time Malachi took place, the storehouse was not the temple, therefore it should not be referred to as the church today.

Let me begin by cutting straight to the chase. Did you know the phrase, "Will a man rob God," (Mal. 3:8), was not directed to the people (congregation) rather to the **priest** (church leadership)? If you are like me, you've never heard anything like this before, but it's actually true. The message from Malachi was directed to corrupt priest in the temple. After I show you this insight, you're going to be appalled because you're going to realize it was right there in front of you the entire time. However, before we get started, please allow me to share this side-note.

SIDE-NOTE COMMENTARY:

Before I begin I want to encourage Christians to do a better job in studying their bibles for themselves. Most Christians believe and support everything their leader says, without verifying it. This is problematic because a significant part of our problems in Christianity is related to doctrinal disagreements from church to church. Every church has a different interpretation of the *same* bible. What's really disturbing is that each of these churches claim to have the "Real" truth. Who's right, I don't quite know, but I can tell you, someone is wrong!

Most of these doctrinal disagreements stem from individuals private interpretations of scriptures. Interpretations that are inconsistent with the true intent of the writer's message. Once again, because people have ignored the purpose of the writer's message, misinterpretation and improper application is common. Now we have numerous scriptures used out of context to support personal agendas and to prove individual perspectives, whether it be good or evil. Did you know slavery was once practiced by some Christians reading the same bible you're reading today? This is a prime example of improper interpretation of scripture which always has the possibility to produce abuse and misuse.

Ignoring the writers' purpose will always lead to improper application, which explains why we have an unacceptable amount of doctrinal errors inside and outside the church. Let me share with you a modern-day example of doctrinal error that derived from scripture misinterpretation. There are churches that have incorporated venomous snakes into their worship experience, this is clearly false doctrine! These churches have taken Luke 10:19 way out of context, "Behold, I give unto you power to tread on serpents and scorpions, and over all the power of the enemy: and nothing shall by any means hurt you." Of course, if you put this verse into its proper context, you'll find Luke the writer was speaking in figurative terms, not literal!

So many Christians are led astray from hearing and believing everything they hear come across the pulpit. My momma, always said, "Be careful whose plate you eat from." Though momma was referring to natural food, this is true of spiritual food as well. We need to be cautious who feeds us spiritual food. In today's church, I've noticed most Christians are genuinely afraid to challenge their leaders and fact-check what they're hearing.

Believing everything you hear come across the pulpit and being afraid to fact-check your leader, can be sometimes be fatal. If you don't believe it can be fatal, look up the, The Jonestown Massacre, led by a wicked "Christian" cult leader, Jim Jones. He persuaded his followers to drink toxic Kool-Aid and give it to their kids as well. He manipulated the bible, and convinced his followers it was God's will – suicide. Hundreds died from drinking this toxic Kool-Aid. What are you drinking from your leader? *Please know some poisons kill gradually. So because you don't see the adverse effects immediately, it doesn't mean your church doctrine is correct.*

The point I'm emphasizing is we need to study, know God for ourselves, and we need to stop allowing everyone tell us what to believe. You don't have to know a lot, however you do need to know enough to know when someone is adding or taking away from the Word.

This is the problem we have with the topic of tithing misinterpretation which has produced improper application. I'm not saying the message of tithing isn't taught and supported by sincere God loving people. I absolutely don't believe that all teachers that teach tithing are deliberately misguiding their followers, however I do believe there are some that are. I believe because Malachi has been misconstrued and misapplied, it has opened the door for financial corruption in the church today; similar to what Malachi was addressing in the temple back then. Now, let's discuss corruption in the temple.

PART 1: CORRUPTION IN THE TEMPLE: WHO'S TO BLAME?

I will prove beginning in Chapter 1 Malachi that this message was regarding the priest, not the people. Ultimately, we will find that Malachi 3:8 message "Will a man rob God" was a message directed to corrupt priest.

Malachi 1:6-14, "⁶ A son honors his father, and a slave his master. If I am a father, where is the honor due me? If I am a master, where is the respect due me?" says the Lord Almighty. **"It is you priests who show contempt for my name. But you ask, 'How have we shown contempt for your name?"** ⁷ "By offering defiled food on my altar. "But **you** ask, 'How have we defiled you? "By saying that the Lord's Table is contemptible. ⁸ When **you** offer blind animals for sacrifice, is that not wrong? When **you** sacrifice lame or diseased animals, is that not wrong? Try offering them to your governor! Would he be pleased with **you**? Would he accept **you**?" says the Lord Almighty. ⁹ "Now plead with God to be gracious to us. With such offerings from your hands, will he accept **you**?"—says the Lord Almighty. ¹⁰ "Oh, that one of **you** would shut the temple doors, so that **you** would not light useless fires on my altar! I am not pleased with **you**," says the Lord Almighty, "and I will accept no offering from your hands. ¹¹ My name will be great among the nations, from where the sun rises to where it sets. In every place incense and pure offerings will be brought to me, because my name will be great among the nations," says the Lord Almighty. ¹² "But **you** profane it by saying, 'The Lord's table is defiled,' and, 'Its food is contemptible.' ¹³ And **you** say, 'What a burden!' and you sniff at it contemptuously," says the Lord Almighty. "When **you** bring injured, lame or diseased animals and offer them as sacrifices, should I accept them from your hands?" says the Lord. ¹⁴ "Cursed is the cheat who has an acceptable male in his flock and vows to give it, but then sacrifices a blemished animal to the Lord. For I am a great king," says the Lord Almighty, "and my name is to be feared among the nations.

Question: Who was the "you" Malachi was directing this message to? No need to speculate, verse 6 provides us the answer, **"It is 'you priests' who show contempt for my name. But you ask, 'How have we shown contempt for your name?"**

Here's a few important observations from this passage:

1) As stated in verse 6 Malachi is speaking to the *priest*. He rebukes the priest, not the people for dishonoring and despising God's name.
2) Notice in verse 7 who responds, The Priest! They said, "Wherein have we despised thy name?" This supports the point who Malachi was directing his rebuke to from the beginning.

3) Nature of rebuke. The priest were giving God the defiled part of the offering. [see v.7,8]
4) Malachi accused them of improperly handling the congregations' offerings.
5) As a result of this misuse and abuse, the curse was impending.

As you have read within our study the Priest served on the behalf of the people of the nation of Israel. The priest were mediators, they stood between God and the people. I want you to notice from the beginning who this conversation is clearly directed to – **the Priest**. The people who I will be referring to as the "Congregation" was not the intended recipient of Malachi's message. Malachi is addressing the priest or as I like to refer to as, "Church leadership".

This message was a stern rebuke to the priest who were accused of despising and dishonoring God in the temple.

Without going into great detail about this rebuke, I will give you a synopsis. The priest were required to give the best portion of the sacrifices as an offering to God on behalf of the people. However instead of honoring God with the best of the best, the priest kept the best parts for themselves, basically leaving God the worse portion - the blind, sick and lame parts.

Let me continue to build this case of, who was Malachi addressing?

Let's continue to prove our claim.

Malachi 2:1 – And now, **O ye priests**, this commandment *is* for **you**.

Here in Chapter 2, once again, Malachi is addressing the "you" – the Priest, not the congregation. Notice what he says in Malachi 2:7-9, "⁷For the lips of a priest ought to preserve knowledge, because he *is* the messenger of the Lord Almighty and people seek instruction from his mouth. ⁸ But you have turned from the way and by your teaching have caused many to stumble; you have violated (**corrupted**) the covenant with Levi," says the Lord Almighty. ⁹ "So I have caused you to be despised and humiliated before all the people, because you have not followed my ways but have shown partiality in matters of the law."

CORRUPTION IN THE TEMPLE:

Now we get into the heart of this rebuke – Corruption. This rebuke was not levied against the people the "congregation". It's apparent they fulfilled their obligation by bringing the tithe and offering to the priest as they were required to do. However, the priest were the ones out of divine order for not doing what they were assigned to do with the congregation's tithes and offerings. Based on verse 8, "But ye are departed out of the way; ye have caused many to stumble at the law; ye have *corrupted* the covenant of Levi, saith the LORD of hosts." Malachi is calling what the priest were doing CORRUPT. They were corrupt because they were stealing God's portion of the tithe and offerings, and they were manipulating the law to justify it.

Is it so hard to believe there was corruption in the temple back then? It shouldn't be. Corruption in the temple was nothing new. The fact is, whenever you have money involved in anything, there is always the possibility of corruption. Take into account it was money that motivated Judas Iscariot to sell Jesus out for thirty pieces of silver. Reference [Matthew 26:15]

It was corruption in the temple that led to Jesus over-turning the tables in the temple, because they were inside hustling. Likewise, here in Malachi the Priest were taking the congregation's portion of the tithe and offerings.

These priests were the ones stealing from God. They justified their theft by manipulating the law to condone their conduct. Sound familiar?

The Priest, church leadership, were the ones that were corrupt. Let's take a look at this corruption in the temple.

Nehemiah 13:1-13, "¹On that day the Book of Moses was read aloud in the hearing of the people and there it was found written that no Ammonite or Moabite should ever be admitted into the assembly of God, ²because they had not met the Israelites with food and water but had hired Balaam to call a curse down on them. (Our God, however, turned the curse into a blessing.) ³When the people heard this law, they excluded from Israel all who were of foreign descent. ⁴Before this, Eliashib the priest had been put in charge of the storerooms of the house of our God. He was closely associated with Tobiah, ⁵and he had provided him with a large room formerly used to store the grain offerings and incense and temple articles, and also the tithes of grain, new wine and olive oil prescribed for the Levites, musicians and gatekeepers, as well as the contributions for the priests. ⁶But while all this was going on, I was not in Jerusalem, for in the thirty-second year of Artaxerxes king of Babylon I had returned to the king. Sometime later I asked his permission ⁷and came back to Jerusalem. Here I learned about the evil thing Eliashib had done in providing Tobiah a room in the courts of the house of God. ⁸I was greatly displeased and threw all Tobiah's household goods out of the room. ⁹I gave orders to purify the rooms, and then I put back into them the equipment of the house of God, with the grain offerings and the incense. ¹⁰I also learned that the portions assigned to the Levites had not been given to them, and that all the Levites and musicians responsible for the service had gone back to their own fields. ¹¹So I rebuked the officials and asked them, "Why is the house of God neglected?" Then I called them together and stationed them at their posts. [12] All Judah brought the tithes of grain, new wine and olive oil into the storerooms. [13] I put Shelemiah the priest, Zadok the scribe, and a Levite named Pedaiah in charge of the storerooms and made Hanan son of Zakkur, the son of Mattaniah, their assistant, because they were considered trustworthy. They were made responsible for distributing the supplies to their fellow Levites.

Allow me to give you a quick breakdown of what's going on here. There are five important observations I'd like to point out from this passage, but the complete breakdown will be provided later in this section.

1) Eliashib was a corrupt priest.
2) Only the priest had access and authority to the storeroom that was inside the temple. [Nehemiah 13:4]
3) The storeroom is not the house of God. The storeroom was inside the house of God, the temple. We will discuss the purpose of this room shortly.
4) There was corruption going on inside the temple.
5) The corruption was perpetrated by the priest.

PART 2: THE STOREHOUSE IS NOT THE CHURCH

I made this a subtopic because I found it necessary to clear up this huge misconception. Have you ever heard the phrase, "Bring ye the tithe and offerings to the storehouse?" Church leaders are guilty of using the terms **storehouse and church** interchangeably. However, it's extremely important for you to understand they aren't the same. Decoding this will significantly help you better understand Malachi Chapter 3 when we get there.

Nehemiah 10:35-39 says, "[35]We also assume responsibility for bringing to the house of the Lord each year the firstfruits of our crops and of every fruit tree. [36] "As it is also written in the Law, we will bring the firstborn of our sons and of our cattle, of our herds and of our flocks to the house of our God, to the priests ministering there. [37] "Moreover, we will bring to the storerooms of the house of our God, to the priests, the first of our ground meal, of our grain offerings, of the fruit of all our trees and of our new wine and olive oil. And we will bring a tithe of our crops to the Levites, for it is the Levites who collect the tithes in all the towns where we work. [38] A priest descended from Aaron is to accompany the Levites when they receive the tithes, and the Levites are to bring a tenth of the tithes up to the house of our God, to the storerooms of the treasury. [39] The people of Israel, including the Levites, are to bring their contributions of grain, new wine and olive oil to the storerooms, where the articles for the sanctuary and for the ministering priests, the gatekeepers and the musicians are also kept. "We will not neglect the house of our God."

Nehemiah 10:38 - A priest descended from Aaron is to accompany the Levites when they receive the tithes, and the Levites are to bring a tenth of the tithes up to the <u>house of our God, to the storerooms of the treasury</u>.

Based upon this verse the storehouse/storeroom is *not* the **same** as the house of God (church). The storehouse/storeroom were sections inside the temple. From my study, I found storehouse and storeroom terminology used interchangeably. They both depict a section 'room' inside the temple. This room was used to store the tithe, offerings, and firstfruits collected from the people in the nation of Israel.

Important fact: The priest were commanded to give the Aaronic priest a tenth of the tithe one-percent and that portion was to be stored inside the storeroom. Verse 38, "A priest descended from Aaron is to accompany the Levites when they receive the tithes, and the Levites are to bring a tenth of the tithes up to the house of our God, to the storerooms of the treasury."

Question: Why would God required (1%) of the tithe to be put aside?

The intended purpose for that one-percent of goods stored in this storeroom was for the temple workers. Verse 39, "The people of Israel, including the Levites, are to bring their contributions of grain, new wine and olive oil to the storerooms, where the articles for the sanctuary and for the ministering priests, the gatekeepers and the musicians are also kept. "We will not neglect the house of our God."

Also Nehemiah 13:5 states, "And he had prepared for him a large room, where previously they had stored the grain offerings, the frankincense, the articles, the tithes of grain, the new wine and oil, which were commanded to be given to the Levites and singers and gatekeepers, and the offerings for the priests."

PART 3: WHO'S REALLY ROBBING GOD?

Corruption in the Temple: The sin of Eliashib the priest.

Now I will explain Nehemiah 13:1-13. When Nehemiah returned to Jerusalem and discovered that Eliashib had been squandering the peoples' offerings, he discovered Eliashib had rented a room in the temple to a gentleman named Tobiah. Rather than take the one-percent of the peoples' offerings required to be stored in the storehouse, he sold them to Tobiah. [Nehemiah 13:6-8]

The priest Eliashib was a crook! The one-percent he was required to take to the storehouse represented God's portion of the tithe. God chose to use that portion for those that worked inside the temple. Eliashib was essentially robbing

God of the opportunity of meeting the needs of the people he wanted to support with this portion. Therefore, not only was he robbing God, he was literally robbing the people God intended to bless with that portion of the tithe and offering. He was corrupt, he stole it and sold it for **self-gain**.

Now that you understand that, you'll now see why Malachi was addressing the priests because they were guilty of this same type of corruption. I wanted you to actually see this example of priest corruption and how it looks, so when we delve back into Malachi, it'll all come together.

Based upon what we've discovered from Chapter 1 and 2, we can easily tell Malachi is speaking to the priest, not the congregation.

Now let's go to the Book of Malachi to see how this all ties together.

Malachi 3:7–10, "⁷ Ever since the time of your ancestors **you** have turned away from my decrees and have not kept them. Return to me, and I will return to **you**," says the Lord Almighty. "But **you** ask, 'How are we to return?' ⁸"Will a mere mortal rob God? Yet **you** rob me. "But **you** ask, 'How are we robbing you?' "In tithes and offerings. ⁹**You** are under a curse—your whole nation because **you** are robbing me. ¹⁰ Bring the whole tithe into the storehouse, that there may be food in my house. Test me in this," says the Lord Almighty, "and see if I will not throw open the floodgates of heaven and pour out so much blessing that there will not be room enough to store it.

Notice here in chapter 3 Malachi refers to message recipients as "You".

Test question: Who was the "you" referring to in both chapter 1 & 2?

A) The people (congregation)
B) The priest (church leadership)
C) Both (the priest and people)

Write your answer here: _____

The correct answer is (B) The priest (church leadership).

Malachi 1:6 NKJV	Malachi 3:8 NKJV
A son honoureth his father, and a servant his master: if then I be a father, where is mine honour? And if I be a master, where is my fear? saith the LORD of hosts unto **YOU**, O priests, that despise my name. And ye say, **Wherein have we despised thy name**?	Will a man rob God? Yet you have robbed Me! But **YOU** say, '**In what way have we robbed You**? In tithes and offerings'.

We see the response to the question asked in Malachi 3:8, "Will a man rob God?" Yet, **you** have robbed me! But

you say, "In what way have we robbed you?" Malachi 1:6 response, "A son honoureth his father, and a servant his master: if then I be a father, where is mine honour? And if I be a master, where is my fear? saith the LORD of hosts unto **you, O priests,** that despise my name. And ye say, Wherein have we despised thy name?"

Please take a minute and view the chart and compare the priest responses.

Aren't both of these dialogues and responses similar?

It is obvious that Malachi was addressing the same people he had been addressing in both Chapter one and two, which were the Priest. They were the "YOU" he was referencing. There's absolutely no evidence of this conversation ever changing from the priest to the congregation or anyone else. The Priest were being rebuked for committing the sin of Eliashib. Like Eliashib's sin of corruption they too were squandering the tithe and offerings, they were robbing God!

The priest were not only robbing God, but also the people God intended to bless through the tithe and offering system. That's why in verse 9 he said, "You have robbed Me, Even this whole nation". What nation is he referring to? The people in the nation of Israel. Remember the tithe and offerings had multiple applications. The Levitical tithe being one for the priest and the other two (festival and poor tithe) was for the people in the nation of Israel. When the priest stole these tithes and offerings they not only stole from God, but the entire nation as well.

It's very imperative to grasp the true point here. God fully expects the blessings to circulate. Today we have people giving all their money to the church which happens to make the (church) preacher prosperous, however this money rarely ever circles back around to the people that are giving. Most churches today sell almost everything to their members. Things such as videos, cd's, banquets, special conferences, kid's camps & programs, the list goes on and on. Everything comes with a cost at most churches today. The leaders preach give to us *now*, but you'll get yours later supernaturally somehow. Its unfortunate most churches disregard teaching people to be financially responsible with their giving. Most people negate being financially responsible just to be so-called "right" with the Lord. However when they find themselves in a financial bind the church oftentimes deny or at times partially assist them through the financial crisis they experience as a result of giving above there means. Most are encouraged to pray for Gods help.

Is your church merely a religious business or a place that seeks to help humanity?

It's difficult to answer this question because rarely is there any true transparency where the money goes. Most church leaders would like us to simply believe the money is taken up by an angel and carried into heaven to God's throne. He then divvy's it out to his children according to their needs. No, the money stays in the earth realm in some bank account with a "man or woman" name on it, and it's not in Jesus' name. Therefore its incumbent that the church leaders don't ROB Gods people by not circulating the money back around to them. My point, God wants the benefits to reach the highest to the lowest.

Back to Malachi Chapter 3.

Take notice to the word *all* in verse 10, it's significant. "Bring ye **all** the tithe and offerings into the storehouse, that there may be food in my house." Notice *all* was stated only because the priest were squandering the (1%) portion earmarked for the storehouse.

The second part of that verse, "That there may be food in my house," notice the distinction of *food in my house*. The house was referring to the storehouse, which is where they stored the food for the temple workers. God was warning these crooked priests to stop stealing the tithe and offerings (food), rather take the full portion "all one-percent" from the storehouse.

Due to the corrupt priesthood in the temple, this increased the risk of significantly impacting the nation. To advert sure judgement, God offered them an out, he said, "Return unto him," and he would return to them. Return to what? His ordinance – order. In so returning to his order, he would bless them as he promised in verses 11 & 12.

Malachi 3:11-12, "I will prevent pests from devouring your crops, and the vines in your fields will not drop their fruit before it is ripe, says the Lord Almighty. Then all the nations will call you blessed, for yours will be a delightful land, says the Lord Almighty."

In conclusion, I would like to leave you with "4" important insights:

1) In Malachi 3:8 he was not directing his comments to the congregation rather the priests (church leaders). Teachers of tithing have primarily used this scripture to invoke FEAR into their member's hearts to tithe consistently. However, once you put Malachi's message into proper context you clearly see this was a message about corrupt priest. Therefore, the question isn't are you (the people) robbing God, rather is our church leadership robbing you and God through the

misuse and abuse of the tithe and offerings you've given?

2) The corrupt priest misuse and abuse of the tithe and offerings opened the door for the curse to come upon the people they led.

3) The tithing system was under the Mosaic Law which is the Old Testament covenant. This covenant was based upon the principle described in Deuteronomy chapter 28.

Deuteronomy 28:1-2 says, "**If** you fully obey the Lord your God and carefully follow all his commands I give you today, the Lord your God will set you high above all the nations on earth. ²All these blessings will come on you and accompany you **if** you obey the Lord your God:

The principle was if you **do** this – God will do that. The blessings and curses of that covenant were on a contingency basis. However, we are no longer under that old covenant. Christ has given us a new covenant with better promises. This covenant isn't based upon if you **do**, rather if you **BELIEVE**! By believing, I mean having FAITH.

Hebrews 8:5-7 states, "⁵They serve at a sanctuary that is a copy and shadow of what is in heaven. This is why Moses was warned when he was about to build the tabernacle: "See to it that you make everything according to the pattern shown you on the mountain." ⁶ But in fact the ministry Jesus has received is as superior to theirs as the covenant of which he is mediator is superior to the old one, since the **new covenant** is established on **better promises**. ⁷For if there had been nothing wrong with that first covenant, no place would have been sought for another.

Under this new covenant, the promises are not based upon works of the law, rather one must believe and have faith. *"But without faith it is impossible to [walk with God and] please Him, for whoever comes [near] to God must [necessarily] believe that God exists and that He rewards those who [earnestly and diligently] seek Him."* [Hebrews 11:6 AMP]

Malachi 3:8 said they were robbing God of, "tithes and offerings." Notice he didn't just say **tithes**. He stated, ***tithe and offerings***. Offering(s) in this verse is plural, meaning 'many'. This observation has been overlooked, however the word offerings is plural for a reason. I'll explain that reason shortly.

<u>It's quite interesting how the requirement ONLY for tithing was pulled from this verse while offering was ignored</u>. Based upon this verse 10, offerings should have been required too. However most teachers only teach – an offering is anything "voluntary offering" that's *above* the tithe the "tenth", however I've never heard them describe the offering as a requirement such as the tithe, rather a "voluntary offering."

For example: If your paycheck was $500, based upon the teaching I've heard you would tithe $50, and then any monetary contribution above the $50 would be considered an offering. This is what some tithing teachers teach regarding giving, however this isn't biblically-based. The offerings in the Book of Malachi were not directly related to a monetary offering.

The term *offerings* has been misconstrued to mean a monetary contribution, however this is not the true meaning of offerings in Malachi 3:8. <u>These offerings were referring to the five types of the major offerings offered in the Old Testament, which were the Burnt Offering, Grain Offering, Peace Offering, Purification Offering, and the Reparation Offering.</u>

1) **Burnt Offering:** The purpose of the Burnt Offering was for general atonement of sin and expression of devotion to God. The instructions for the Burnt Offering are given in Leviticus 1:3-17. The offering could be a bull (1:3), sheep or goat (1:10), or a dove or pigeon (1:14). The animal was to be burnt whole overnight (6:8-13), yet its skin was given to the priest (1:6).

2) **Grain Offering:** The purpose of the Grain Offering was a voluntary expression of devotion to God, recognizing His goodness and providence. The instructions for the grain offerings are given in Leviticus 2:4-14. Generally, it was cooked

bread—baked (2:4), grilled (2:5), fried (2:7), roasted, or made into cereal (2:14)—though always seasoned (2:13), unsweetened, and unleavened (2:11). Unlike the whole Burnt Offering, only a portion of the offering was to be burnt (2:9). The remainder went to the priests for their meal (2:10).

3) **Peace Offering**: This category, first discussed in Leviticus 3, included Thanksgiving Offerings (Lev 7:11, 12), Freewill Offerings (7:15-16), and Wave Offerings (7:30). The offering could be cattle (3:1), sheep (3:7), or a goat (3:12). It could be male or female, but had to be without defect. If it was a Thanksgiving Offering, it could also include a variety of breads (7:12). The purpose of the Peace Offering was to consecrate a meal between two or more parties before God, and share that meal together in fellowship of peace and a commitment to each other's future prosperity. The portions unsuitable for eating were given to God (7:19-27). Depending on the type of Peace Offering, the breast may have been given to the High Priest (7:31) and the right thigh may be given to the priest officiating the meal (7:32). The rest of the meal was to be eaten within one day by the fellowship of parties (7:16), and the leftovers were to be burnt after two days (7:17).

4) **Sin Offering**: This offering is sometimes seen as an offering of atonement for unintentional sin

(4:2-3, 4:20). Similarly, it is sometimes viewed as guilt offering, removing the consequences for lack of perfection (4:13-14, 4:22-23). As an atonement offering, it contained elements of a Burnt offering (4:25). Yet, at the same time had elements of a Peace offering (4:26). Conversely, some of the sins for which one needed atonement were not moral sins, but rather matters of ritual impurity (5:1-5). As such, some have proposed the term Purification Offering, instead of Sin Offering. The primary purpose of this offering is not to atone for sins, but rather to purify oneself for re-entering the presence of God. The elements of a Purification Offering could be any of the elements of the previous three types of offerings. Though unlike the Peace Offering, the meal was not to be shared by the one offering the sacrifice.

5) **Trespass Offering**: The purpose of this offering was to make reparations for one's sin. As such, this offering had a specific monetary value, and one who *owed* another on account of a debt due to a "sin" could repay it in silver rather than by sacrificing a ram (5:15). In addition, a twenty-percent fee was assessed and given to the priest who mitigated the debt (5:16). *Note: Money was only used if a debt was owed.*

These offerings were primarily agricultural produce and livestock, not money. Money was only used for repayment of debt under the Trespass Offering.

Basically, the priests were not only guilty of stealing the tithes, but also the offerings. Now that we have put this book into proper context, hopefully you realize this offering was not referring to monetary contributions, rather the offerings offered under the old covenant law. Kind of ironic this hasn't been taught this way. **Lastly, consider this, if we're required to tithe based upon Malachi 3:8, shouldn't we also be required to give offerings as well?** Remember Malachi 3:8 says, "Will a man rob God? Yet you have robbed Me! But you say, 'In what way have we robbed you? In tithes and offerings." **Notice it didn't just say they were robbing God of the tithes, but also the offerings as well.**

The two take-away points from the Book of Malachi:

1) Malachi message wasn't directed to the people 'the congregation', rather to the priest 'church leadership'.

2) During this period of time tithes and offerings were practiced under the Old Testament 'Law of Moses'.

Chapter 4

JESUS ON TITHING: WAS IT TAUGHT OR COMMANDED?

PART 1: DID JESUS TEACH, COMMAND OR ENDORSE TITHING IN THE NEW TESTAMENT?

This chapter is extremely important in establishing the fact tithing is not a New Testament requirement. It never fails when someone is attempting to prove why we should tithe in the New Testament, they only have only one single reference from Jesus to point to. So during my research on this subject, I carefully examined this reference of tithing made by Jesus. I'm going to tell you upfront what I found from my research, and this study will consist of the actual proof to support my point of view.

The reference in question:

Luke 11:37-44 states, "³⁷And as He spoke, a certain Pharisee asked Him to dine with him. So He went in and sat down to eat. ³⁸ When the Pharisee saw *it*, he marveled that He had not first washed before dinner.³⁹ Then the Lord said to him, "Now you Pharisees make the outside of the cup and dish clean, but your inward part is full of greed and wickedness. ⁴⁰ Foolish ones! Did not He who made the outside make the inside also? ⁴¹But rather give alms of such things as you have; then indeed all things are clean to you. ⁴² "But woe to you Pharisees! For you tithe mint and rue and all manner of herbs, and pass by justice and the love of God. These you ought to have done, without leaving the others undone. ⁴³Woe to you Pharisees! For you love the best seats in the synagogues and greetings in the marketplaces. ⁴⁴Woe to you, scribes and Pharisees, hypocrites! For you are like graves which are not seen, and the men who walk over *them* are not aware *of them*."

What I would like you to understand is that Jesus' comments here pertaining to tithing was NOT him making a New Testament command or endorsement to tithing. This comment was solely about a religious Pharisee that gave alms and tithes yet ignored the condition of his heart. The fact is Jesus never taught, commanded or even endorsed tithing and I will prove it in this part of our study.

Let me begin by asking you a question, have you ever questioned that if tithing was so critical why didn't Jesus teach and require his disciples to follow this principle? Considering tithing is so crucial in most churches today, how could this principle go ignored by Jesus? Tithing has literally become a tenet of our faith. It's fair to say to be considered a Christian in some church circles, you must get saved and you must tithe thereafter.

In some churches tithing has become a tenet of their faith!

Common consequences if you don't tithe:

1) You can't operate in any capacity of leadership in most churches.
2) Oftentimes you will be disqualified from financial assistance from most churches, because you're deemed living under a closed heaven for stealing Gods money.
3) As a result of stealing God's money, anything bad that happens to you is likely attributed to not tithing, therefore many won't help you or even pray for you.

The tithing message today describes people who don't tithe as thieves for stealing God's money. It suggests because they are stealing his tithe, he's angry and has abandoned them by leaving them to contend in this life alone without his help, they're "Cursed with a curse."

Many people who struggle to tithe are left feeling guilty and condemned. Can you blame them? Who wants God against them when the whole world already is? Who can have a clear conscience toward a God when you believe you've stolen from him?

This is absolutely why we need to address the question whether or not Jesus taught tithing.

Let's begin.

Our operative verse in this passage is verse 42.

(42) <u>But woe unto you, Pharisees! For ye tithe mint and rue and all manner of herbs, and pass over judgment and the love of God: these ought ye to have done, and not to leave the other undone</u>.

Whenever the question is posed, did Jesus teach tithing or endorse tithing in the New Testament? Advocates of tithing say, yes, and they use this verse to support their persuasion. I'm sure from first sight you may be thinking it does look like an endorsement from Jesus, however, I will show you that in fact this was not a New Testament endorsement of tithing.

In order to explain the source of where this confusion all stems from, it's paramount you know when the Old Testament *ends* and the New Testament *begins*. Many people are aware that the four gospels (Matthew, Mark,

Luke & John) recorded the birth, life and death of Jesus. However, what they fail to realize is that until Jesus died, they still operated under the Old Testament covenant practices – the Mosaic Law. You must understand this fundamental truth in order to understand a lot of things about the bible. I will take a moment and explain this biblical fact, then I'll address the original question, "Did Jesus teach or endorse tithing in the New Testament?"

Important Fact: Until Jesus died, the people operated under the Old Testament law.

PART 2: WHEN DID THE OLD TESTAMENT END AND NEW TESTAMENT BEGIN?

I marvel at the number of people that call themselves scholars of the Word, yet are unaware of this fundamental truth. I'm not attempting to be overly critical. I'm just concerned if this fundamental truth isn't understood it becomes the basis of bible misunderstanding.

When I realized people didn't understand when the Old Testament ends and the New Testament begins, I finally understood why so many people still practiced Old Testament practices, such as tithing. So if you were one of the ones who don't quite know the answer to the question, when the Old Testament ends and the New Testament actually begins, I'm glad you're reading this book, because you will learn today.

So when did the New Testament begin? Normally when I ask this question, I generally get one of these three answers:

A. The birth of Jesus
B. The death of Jesus
C. Book of Acts – "The Day of Pentecost "

So if I ask you the same question, "When did the New Testament begin?" Which answer would you choose? Take a minute and decide before reading further.

Okay, hopefully you got your answer. If you selected option A or C you'd be wrong. The correct answer is B.

Let me prove this.

Notice what the Old Testament Prophet Jeremiah prophesied:

Jeremiah 31:31- Behold, the days come, saith the LORD, that I will make a *new covenant* with the house of Israel, and with the house of Judah:

He said, "The Lord was going to make a NEW covenant." So when did the Lord make this new covenant?

Did this covenant go into effect when Jesus was born in the manger? No, Jesus's birth alone didn't ratify the new covenant. So did the new covenant go into effect on the day of Pentecost in the book of Acts? Technically, no, it didn't go into effect at the time, it was already in effect.

The new covenant was ratified when Jesus shed his Blood – his death.

Hebrews 10:5-9 NIV, "⁵ Therefore, when Christ came into the world, he said: "Sacrifice and offering you did not desire, but a body you prepared for me; ⁶ with burnt offerings and sin offerings you were not pleased. ⁷ Then I said, 'Here I am—it is written about me in the scroll—I have come to do your will, my God. ⁸ First he said, "Sacrifices and offerings, burnt offerings and sin offerings you did not desire, nor were you pleased with them"—though they were offered in accordance with the law. ⁹ Then he said, "Here I am, I have come to do your will." He sets aside the first to establish the second.

Hebrews 10:9 NKJV says, "Then He said, "Behold, I have come to do Your will, O God." He takes away the first that He may establish the second.

It states, "He" referring to Christ will **take away** the first referring to covenant or testament that he may establish the second covenant/testament.

Now let's prove that point.

Hebrews 9:14-28 NIV says, "[14] how much more shall the blood of Christ, who through the eternal Spirit offered Himself without spot to God, cleanse your conscience from dead works to serve the living God? [15]**And for this reason He is the Mediator <u>of the new covenant, by means of death</u>**, for the redemption of the transgressions under the first covenant, that those who are called may receive the promise of the eternal inheritance. [16] <u>**For where there *is* a testament, there must also of necessity be the death of the testator.**</u> [17]For a testament *is* in force after men are dead, since it has no power at all while the testator lives. [18] Therefore not even the first *covenant* was dedicated without blood. [19]For when Moses had spoken every precept to all the people according to the law, he took the blood of calves and goats, with water, scarlet wool, and hyssop, and sprinkled both the book itself and all the people, [20]saying, "This *is* the blood of the covenant which God has commanded you." [21] Then likewise he sprinkled with blood both the tabernacle and all the vessels of the ministry. [22] And according to the law almost all things are purified with blood, and without shedding of blood there is no remission. [23] Therefore *it was* necessary that the copies of the things in the heavens should be purified with these, but the heavenly things themselves with better sacrifices than these. [24]For Christ has not entered the holy places made with hands, *which are* copies of the true, but into heaven itself, now to appear in the presence of God for us; ²⁵not that He should offer Himself often, as the high priest enters the Most Holy Place every year with blood of another— ²⁶ He then would have had to suffer often since the foundation of the world; but now, once at the end of the ages, He has appeared to put away sin by the sacrifice of Himself. ²⁷And as it is appointed for men to die once, but after this the judgment, ²⁸so Christ was offered once to bear the sins of many. To those who eagerly wait for Him He will appear a second time, apart from sin, for salvation.

Notice the word *testator* in verse 16. A testator is a person who has written and executed a last will and testament that is in effect at the time of his/her death.

After reading this there should be no questions or doubts about when the New Testament begins. It began *after* Jesus Christ shed his Blood on Calvary – his death.

Hebrews 9:15-17 AMP

¹⁵For this reason He is the Mediator *and* Negotiator of a new covenant [that is, an entirely new agreement uniting God and man], so that those who have been called [by God] may receive [the fulfillment of] the promised eternal inheritance, since a death has taken place [as the payment] which redeems them from the sins *committed* under the *obsolete* first covenant. ¹⁶**For where there is a will *and* testament involved, the death of the one who made it**

must be established, **¹⁷for a will _and_ testament takes effect [only] at death**, since it is never in force as long as the one who made it is alive.

Let me give you an outline of our main points:

1) The testator is none other than Jesus
2) The WILL is the New Testament / New Covenant
3) The New Testament (covenant) became effective when Jesus died on the cross. His blood ratified this new covenant.

Matthew 27:45-51, "Now from the sixth hour (noon) there was darkness over all the land until the ninth hour (3:00 p.m.). About the ninth hour Jesus cried out with a loud [agonized] voice, "Eli, Eli, lama sabachthani?" that is, "My God, My God, why have You forsaken Me?" When some of the bystanders there heard it, they _began_ saying, "This man is calling for Elijah." Immediately one of them ran, and took a sponge, soaked it with sour wine and put it on a reed, and gave Him a drink. But the rest said, "Let us see whether Elijah will come to save Him [from death]." And Jesus cried out again with a loud [agonized] voice, and gave up His spirit [voluntarily, sovereignly dismissing and releasing His spirit from His body in submission to His Father's plan]. And [at once] the veil [of the Holy of Holies] of the temple was torn in two from top to bottom; the earth shook and the rocks were split apart.

John's account of Jesus' death. In John 19:30 he states, "When Jesus had received the sour wine, He said, "**It is finished**!" And He bowed His head and [voluntarily] *gave up His spirit.*

So, Jesus' last statement before he died indicates his earthly assignment was finished. It's important to point out again that up until this point the Law was still in effect. Jesus didn't come to end the Law, his purpose was to fulfill it.

Matthew 5:17 says, "Do not think that I came to do away with *or* undo the Law [of Moses] or the [writings of the] Prophets; I did not come to destroy but to fulfill.

Now that Jesus has fulfilled the Law through his death, the old covenant is now *obsolete*!

Hebrews 9:15 - For this reason He is the Mediator *and* Negotiator of a new covenant [that is, an entirely new agreement uniting God and man], so that those who have been called [by God] may receive [the fulfillment of] the promised eternal inheritance, since a *death* has taken place [as the payment] which redeems them from the sins *committed* under the ***OBSOLETE*** first covenant.

If we are completely free from the law, so why are some practicing any parts of it? *Selah*

In Him you were also circumcised with a circumcision not made with hands, but by the [spiritual] circumcision of Christ in the stripping off of the body of the flesh [the sinful carnal nature], having been buried with Him in baptism and raised with Him [to a new life] through [your] faith in the working of God, [as displayed] when He raised Christ from the dead. When you were dead in your sins and in the uncircumcision of your flesh (worldliness, manner of life), God made you alive together with Christ, having [freely] forgiven us all our sins, having canceled out the certificate of debt consisting of legal demands [which were in force] against us and which were hostile to us. And this certificate He has set aside *and* completely removed by nailing it to the cross. When He had disarmed the rulers and authorities [those supernatural forces of evil operating against us], He made a public example of them [exhibiting them as captives in His triumphal procession], having triumphed over them through the cross. Therefore let no one judge you in regard to food and drink or in regard to [the observance of] a festival or a new moon or a Sabbath day. Such things are only a shadow of what is to come *and* they have only symbolic value; but the substance [the reality of what is foreshadowed] belongs to Christ. Colossians 2:11-17 AMP

Let's return to our original question, did Jesus teach or endorse tithing in the New Testament? Before we dig deeper into our study addressing this question, I want you to take a minute and reread Luke 11:37-44, please pay special attention to verse [42].

Jesus says in verse 42, "*But woe unto you, Pharisees! For ye tithe mint and rue and all manner of herbs, and pass over judgment and the love of God: these ought ye to have done, and not to leave the other undone.*"

Its importance to point out that Jesus was directing this rebuke to the Pharisees.

Who were the Pharisees? The Pharisees were members of an ancient Jewish sect, distinguished by strict observance of the traditional and written law, and commonly held to have pretensions to superior sanctity. Now given the breakdown of what a Pharisee is, let's put this conversation into perspective.

During this period of time that Jesus commented to the Pharisees, the Old Testament law was still in effect, therefore tithing mint and rue and all manner of herbs was proper. So bear in mind what you learned, that the New Testament covenant didn't go into effect until after Jesus died. Therefore, since this rebuke was before his death, Jesus had absolutely no reason at this point to rebuke them on the act of tithing, because tithing at this time was a requirement under the law. Remember, Jesus didn't come to destroy the law or the prophets, he came to *fulfill it*. Jesus rebuke was totally unrelated to their faithful adherence to the law in giving *alms* (v.41) and *tithes* (v.42), he said, "But rather give alms of such things as ye have; and, behold, all things are clean unto you. But woe unto you, Pharisees! For ye tithe mint and rue and all manner of herbs, and pass over judgment and the love of God: these ought ye to have done, and not to leave the other undone."

Jesus rebuke here was directly related to the condition of their hearts in giving the alms and tithes. The rebuke was they were not giving from the heart, they gave only because they were religious. Religious people give, attend church, and serve God publicly only because they are required to, not because their hearts are into it. I once heard, "Who you are publicly isn't the real you." God isn't looking at our external acts, rather our internal motivations.

Furthermore, it's clear to see this was an Old Testament act of tithing simply by *what* he tithed, "*Mint and Rue and all Manner of Herbs.*" **If the church truly wants to use this as an example of New Testament tithing, that would essentially mean we can substitute monetary tithing for other things such as mint, rue, and all manner of herbs aligning with what the Pharisees tithed**.

Is it safe to assume no church would be open to accepting those goods? After all, most churches teach only money is an acceptable form of tithing.

We can easily see this tithing example was definitely an Old Testament practice, and is irrelevant to the New Testament church. Jesus' statement was only intended to point out the major concern he had with the Pharisees – the religious folk that followed external religious practices, yet, ignored the internal condition of their hearts. Jesus was basically saying to the Pharisees, yes you are meeting all the legalistic external practices of the law, however you fail miserably to follow God's righteous internal practice of love and justice.

"God is not concerned with the act of giving alone, rather the condition of our hearts in giving"

So did Jesus teach or endorse tithing in the New Testament? No, he didn't. Let me provide you with one final point that should help solidify this point.

Do you recall when I provided you with the definition of a Pharisee? Remember the Pharisees were highly respected for their strict observance of the traditional and written law. You can see that demonstrated here in Luke 11:42 when the Pharisees gave alms and tithes. Did you know the Apostle Paul who wrote more than half of the New Testament was a Pharisee?

Paul states in Philippians 3:4-6 NIV, "Though I myself have reasons for such confidence. If someone else thinks they have reasons to put confidence in the flesh, I have more: circumcised on the eighth day, of the people of Israel, of the tribe of Benjamin, a Hebrew of Hebrews; **in regard to the law, a Pharisee**; as for zeal, persecuting the church; as for righteousness based on the law, faultless.

Important insight: Paul was a Pharisee and is noted for writing two-thirds of the New Testament. Most of what you believe as a Christian-believer derives from his letters to the church. Prior to Paul's conversion from Judaism, he didn't believe in Christianity, he was a strict follower the Judaic Law. Paul was so convinced Christians were blaspheming, he persecuted them. After his conversion, Paul would become one the most passionate preachers of Jesus Christ in the New Testament. He preached that Christ freed him from the law he once served.

Rhetorical question: If Paul was considered among the greatest of the Pharisees sect due to his zeal and commitment to follow the Law of God, why didn't he tithe, request tithe, teach or endorse tithing, or better yet, mention tithing to any of his churches in the New Testament? Either he forgot or it wasn't a New Testament requirement. Selah

For my bible scholars, it's important to note that the Apostle Paul didn't write the Book of Hebrews, where tithing is only mentioned in the New Testament, yet not commanded. I will address Hebrews 7 in the next chapter in order to discuss in more detail.

PART 3: JESUS' PERSPECTIVE ON MONEY.

It's very unfortunate that the 21st century church has treated tithing like a night club cover charge. I'm not saying giving to the church isn't right, I'm really not. *Actually giving to the church is biblical and should be embraced as a fundamental Christian principle.* However, I'm saying even though giving to church is imperative, there's no specific amount or percentage we're required to give. In reality, God doesn't need your money in Heaven. Money shows him where your heart is at on earth. Matthew 6:21, "For where your treasure is, there your heart will be also."

Jesus' perspective on money wasn't what we hear from some of the prosperity messages taught today. These messages suggest God wants us all rich and the way we receive his riches is by giving to get.

That description encapsulates the message of prosperity we often hear today, which wasn't the message from Jesus on money at all. His message was, make God our source and his purpose on earth our priority and he'll take care of us.

1) Our Source:

   Money is powerful. It has the potential to corrupt the most honest person if they're not careful. Jesus taught we shouldn't live our lives here on earth in pursuit of riches.

"What good is it for someone to gain the whole world, yet forfeit their soul? Or what can anyone give in exchange for their soul?" Mark 8:36-37

In Luke we find a gentleman who didn't make God his source, rather his possessions. This parable is a great example of what it means to strive to gain the world and lose our souls in the process.

Luke 12:13–23 NIV states, "Someone in the crowd said to him, "Teacher, tell my brother to divide the inheritance with me." Jesus replied, "Man, who appointed me a judge or an arbiter between you?" Then he said to them, "**Watch out! Be on your guard against all kinds of greed; life does not consist in an abundance of possessions**." And he told them this parable: "The ground of a certain rich man yielded an abundant harvest. He thought to himself, 'What shall I do? I have no place to store my crops. "Then he said, 'This is what I'll do. I will tear down my barns and build bigger ones, and there I will store my surplus grain. And I'll say to myself, "You have plenty of grain laid up for many years. Take life easy; eat, drink and be merry. But God said to him, 'You fool! This very night your life will be demanded from you. Then who will get what you have prepared for yourself? This is how it will be with whoever stores up things for themselves but is not rich toward God."

Jesus warns us here of covetousness - GREED!

Luke 12:15 NKJV says, "And he said unto them, Take heed, and beware of covetousness: for a man's life consisteth not in the abundance of the things which he possesseth."

Covetousness means having or showing a strong desire for something, especially material possessions. Covetousness is rooted in greed. God doesn't want us driven by greed. He desires us to be content, trusting him as our ultimate source and provider.

Matthew 6:25-32, "Therefore I tell you, do not worry about your life, what you will eat or drink; or about your body, what you will wear. Is not life more than food, and the body more than clothes? Look at the birds of the air; they do not sow or reap or store away in barns, and yet your heavenly Father feeds them. Are you not much more valuable than they? Can any one of you by worrying add a single hour to your life? "And why do you worry about clothes? See how the flowers of the field grow. They do not labor or spin. Yet I tell you that not even Solomon in all his splendor was dressed like one of these. If that is how God clothes the grass of the field, which is here today and tomorrow is thrown into the fire, will he not much more clothe you—you of little faith? So do not worry, saying, 'What shall we eat?' or 'What shall we drink?' or 'What shall we wear?' For the pagans run after all these things, and your heavenly Father knows that you need them.

2) Our Priority

Jesus taught that God should be our priority.

Matthew 6:33 says, "But seek **first** the kingdom of God and His righteousness, and all these things shall be added to you."

God desires us to make kingdom business our earthly priority. By kingdom business I mean supporting his earthly mission through spreading the gospel and helping those that need help. *God expects us to give to this mission commensurable to how he has prospered us.*

These two points aren't intended to be a comprehensive study on Jesus teaching on money, only a general perspective.

Jesus' desire is for us to have possessions, he didn't intend for possessions to have our hearts. It's important to note that individual possessions will vary from individual to individual, so please don't compare yourself to others. Nevertheless it's fair to say you'll likely prosper in accordance to what you can handle, and also according to his plan and purpose for your life. 3 John verse 2 says, "Beloved, I wish above all things that thou mayest prosper and be in health, even as thy soul prospereth." God will not give you anything that will harm you or cause you to lose focus. The statement, more money more problems, can be true if you're not ready for certain possessions and levels of prosperity. Receiving them prematurely can ruin you. Read the story of the Prodigal Son if you don't believe me [Luke 15:11-32].

It's only a test! God wants to know if money is your source and priority or if He is. Oftentimes before he promotes you to another level of prosperity, a test will precede.

Matthew 19:16-22, "Just then a man came up to Jesus and asked, Teacher, what good thing must I do to get eternal life? Why do you ask me about what is good? Jesus replied. There is only one who is good. If you want to enter life, keep the commandments. Which ones? He inquired. Jesus replied, you shall not murder, you shall not commit adultery, you shall not steal, and you shall not give false testimony, honor your father and mother, and love your neighbor as yourself. All these I have kept, the young man said. What do I still lack? Jesus answered, if you want to be perfect, go, sell your possessions and give to the poor, and you will have treasure in heaven. Then come, follow me. When the young man heard this, he went away sad, because he had great wealth."

Here we see a rich guy had a reverential fear for God since he was young, yet when Jesus gave him the money test, he failed. As I said before, God doesn't need our money in heaven, money serves as an indicator to show where our hearts are on earth. Jesus wasn't after this man's fortune, the point he was showing the rich guy was that his possessions had his heart.

While Jesus never taught tithing, he did teach and does expect us to have a heart for God's purpose on earth and give in support of that purpose.

Matthew 22:15-21, "¹⁵Then the Pharisees went and plotted how they might entangle Him in *His* talk. ¹⁶And they sent to Him their disciples with the Herodians, saying, "Teacher, we know that You are true, and teach the way of God in truth; nor do You care about anyone, for You do not regard the person of men. ¹⁷Tell us, therefore, what do You think? *Is it lawful to pay taxes to Caesar, or not?*" ¹⁸But Jesus perceived their wickedness, and said, "Why do you test Me, *you* hypocrites? ¹⁹Show Me the tax money." So they brought Him a denarius. ²⁰And He said to them, "Whose image and inscription *is* this?" ²¹They said to Him, "Caesar's." And He said to them, "Render therefore

<u>to Caesar the things that are Caesar's, and to God the things that are God's."</u>

In particular, verse 21 has also been in the center of many tithing debates. Some advocates of tithing have suggested that this verse depicts the principle of tithing. Once again, that is not true! Once we put this story into its proper context you'll clearly see that Jesus wasn't speaking in code about tithing.

Let me explain the back-story. During this time in history the Jews had been taken over by the Roman Empire, who was led by a wicked emperor name Caesar. So when Jesus stated, "Render therefore to Caesar the things that as Caesar's", he meant just that. During this time the Jews had accepted the rule of the Roman government. As a result of being under this government they were entitled the right to tax them, therefore Jesus said render to Caesar what is due to Caesar.

Although Jesus validated compliance to governmental rules and regulation, he also advocated giving to God by stating we should render to God what belongs to God.

Rendering to Caesar meant paying taxes. What was Jesus referring to when he said they should, render unto God, what's due to him? I can tell you what he was not talking about, and that's tithing. As we learned earlier in our study, tithing was not money, it was agricultural produce and livestock. When Jesus was referencing give money to the temple ['to God'], he was referring to paying the "**temple tax**".

Rendering to Caesar	Rendering to God
"paying governmental taxes"	"paying temple taxes"

Matthew 17:24-27, "After Jesus and his disciples arrived in Capernaum, the collectors of the two-drachma **temple tax** came to Peter and asked, "Doesn't your teacher pay the temple tax?" "Yes, he does," he replied. When Peter came into the house, Jesus was the first to speak. "What do you think, Simon?" he asked. "From whom do the kings of the earth collect duty and taxes—from their own children or from others?" "From others," Peter answered. "Then the children are exempt," Jesus said to him. "But so that we may not cause offense, go to the lake and throw out your line. Take the first fish you catch; open its mouth and you will find a four-drachma coin. Take it and give it to them for my tax and yours."

What is the temple tax? The temple tax was a tax required from Jewish males over the age twenty, and the money was used for the upkeep and maintenance of the temple. [Ex. 30:11-16; 2 Kings 12:5-17; Neh. 10:32-33]

Here in this passage we see Jesus demonstrated giving to God's purpose here on earth. He paid both his and Peter's Temple tax. Matthew 17:27 "But so that we may not cause offense, go to the lake and throw out your line. Take the first fish you catch; open its mouth and you will find a four-drachma coin. **Take it and give it to them for my tax and yours."**

Consider this question. If we're required to pay tithes in the New Testament, then why aren't we requiring the temple tax as well? Jesus paid his and Peter's. The reason the New Testament church don't require temple tax today is the exact reason we shouldn't require the tithe, because both were requirements under the Old Testament covenant.

I hope you have a solid understanding of Jesus Christ's perspective on giving. I wanted to be extremely clear about the point that while Jesus never taught or endorsed New Testament tithing, he did teach and demonstrate making God our priority and source. Wherefore we should give to his purpose here on earth through the church. Now that you know you're not required to tithe in the New Testament, it's vitally important to share with the true way of giving under this new covenant. We'll cover the New Testament way of giving in Chapter 6.

Chapter 5

TITHING IN THE NEW TESTAMENT

PART 1: INTRODUCTION: NEW PRIESTHOOD – NEW LAW AND ORDER

Here in Chapter 5 we will examine specifically what the New Testament says about tithing. In Chapter 4 we learned the New Testament didn't officially begin until the death of Jesus, wherefore Jesus operated under the Old Testament law. It's extremely important for me to note that prior to his death only his chosen people "The Jews", were able to be in covenant with God. However, now because of his death on the cross, everyone can enter into covenant with God. Galatians 3:26-28 says, "For you are all sons of God through faith in Christ Jesus. For as many of you as were baptized into Christ have put on Christ. There is neither Jew nor Greek, there is neither bond nor free, there is neither male nor female: for ye are all one in Christ Jesus." This covenant is called the New Covenant.

Galatians 4:4-7, "But when the set time had fully come, God sent his Son, born of a woman, born under the law, to redeem those under the law, that we might receive adoption to sonship. Because you are his sons, God sent the Spirit of his Son into our hearts, the Spirit who calls out, *"Abba*, Father." So you are no longer a slave, but God's child; and since you are his child, God has made you also an heir."

The bible tells us that Christ has redeemed us from the law. According to Galatians 4:5 says, "To redeem those under the law, that we might receive adoption to sonship. This implies we were adopted into the family of God and were made heirs. What is an heir? An heir is a person legally entitled to the property or rank of another upon a person's death. Essentially when Christ died for us he *willed* us his property and rank.

His Property – the promises of the New Covenant
His Rank – we are now "ALL" the sons of God

Now that we have this new covenant we don't follow the same Levitical order as they did in the Old Testament Law. We no longer need a *living priest* in the New Testament to represent us before God in order to offer the various sacrifices prescribed by the law. There are no sacrifices needed because Jesus was the final sacrifice, and is now our eternal High Priest.

Important-fact: Pastors are not New Testament replacements or substitutes for Old Testament priests.

As you have learned, priests were responsible for representing the people before God. Contrary to what many believe, pastors don't represent us before God. The bible indicates, each individual can have direct access to the throne of God and represent themselves. Hebrews 4:16 says, "Let us therefore come boldly to the throne of grace, that we may obtain mercy and find grace to help in time of need." Don't get me wrong, pastors have tremendous responsibilities, none of which includes representing us before God.

Many people grossly misconstrue the role of the pastor. They mistakenly compare them to the Old Testament priests. I'm convinced this is why so many pastors are overwhelmed. Members expect their pastors to pray for them, study for them and divinely direct their lives. A pastor that fails to teach their members they are not their **mediator,** will find themselves operating outside the grace of Gods help. The primary role of the pastor is to, "shepherd, oversee, lead, and care" for the people God has entrusted them. 1 Peter 5:2, 3 says," Shepherd the flock of God which is among you, serving as overseers, not by compulsion but willingly, not for **dishonest gain** but eagerly; nor as being lords over those entrusted to you, but being examples to the flock.

The reason I distinguished the difference between the pastor and priest is because many believe giving tithes to their pastor is acceptable, when it is not. In the Old Testament God instructed the priest to receive tithes from the people on his behalf. Nowhere in the New Testament will you find God instructing a pastor to receive the tithe on God's behalf.

I must tell you, while the pastor's role is an important role to the church, please understand there are other roles that are just as critical. According to Ephesians Christ has provided the church with what some commonly call the fivefold ministry.

Ephesians 4:11-13

(11) And he gave some, **apostles**; and some, **prophets**; and some, **evangelists**; and some, **pastors** and **teachers**;

(12) For the perfecting of the saints, for the work of the ministry, for the edifying of the body of Christ:

(13) Till we all come in the unity of the faith, and of the knowledge of the Son of God, unto a perfect

man, unto the measure of the stature of the fullness of Christ:

The New Testament five-fold ministry would include the offices' of the apostle, prophet, evangelist, pastor and teacher. Each of these offices are crucial to the body of Christ and neither should be held in less esteem than the other. Please don't get so wrapped up in one over the other such as the Christians did in the Church of Corinth. 1 Corinthians 1:10-13 says, "Now I beseech you, brethren, by the name of our Lord Jesus Christ, that ye all speak the same thing, and that there be no divisions among you; but that ye be perfectly joined together in the same mind and in the same judgment. For it hath been declared unto me of you, my brethren, by them which are of the house of Chloe, that there are contentions among you. Now this I say, that every one of you saith, I am of Paul; and I of Apollos; and I of Cephas; and I of Christ. Is Christ divided? was Paul crucified for you? or were ye baptized in the name of Paul?" 1 Corinthians 3:3-9, "for you are still carnal. For where *there are* envy, strife, and divisions among you, are you not carnal and behaving like *mere* men? For when one says, "I am of Paul," and another, "I *am* of Apollos," are you not carnal? Who then is Paul, and who *is* Apollos, but ministers through whom you believed, as the Lord gave to each one? I planted, Apollos watered, but God gave the increase. So then neither he who plants is anything, nor he who waters, but God who gives the increase. Now he who plants and he who waters are one, and each one will receive his own reward according to his own labor. For we are God's fellow workers; you are God's field, *you are* God's building."

Despite our gift and office we operate in, we are all co-laborers with God. One plants, the other waters but it's ultimately God who provides the results, so he gets all the glory! It's designed that way, so we can't boast or brag.

The point is the pastor is simply one of the five offices God has given to the church, therefore if tithing was prescribed/**commanded,** God would have to described/**instructed** who the tithe should be presented to; the apostle, prophet, evangelist, pastor or teacher. Going forward, please no longer consider or treat your pastor as your priest – liaison to God. Understand under this new and better covenant, Christ has made all believers priests. You can pray, study and get God's guidance for yourself. 1 Peter 2:9 says, "But you are a chosen people,(A) **a royal priesthood,**(B) a holy nation,(C) God's special possession,(D) that you may declare the praises of him who called you out of darkness into his wonderful light." Revelations 1:5-6 says, "And from Jesus Christ, the faithful witness, the firstborn from the dead, and the ruler over the kings of the earth. To Him who loved us and washed us from our sins in His own blood, and has made us kings and **priests** to His God and Father, to Him *be* glory and dominion forever and ever Amen." You don't need a pastor or priest to mediate on your behalf, Christ is your mediator! 1 Timothy 2:5 says, "For *there is* one God, and one mediator between God and men, the man Christ Jesus."

Hebrews 8:1-13 says, "Now the main point of what we are saying is this: We do have such a high priest, who sat down at the right hand of the throne of the Majesty in heaven, and who serves in the sanctuary, the true tabernacle set up by the Lord, not by a mere human being. Every high priest is appointed to offer both gifts and sacrifices, and so it was necessary for this one also to have something to offer. If he were on earth, he would not be a priest, for there are already priests who offer the gifts prescribed by the law. They serve at a sanctuary that is a copy and shadow of what is in heaven. This is why Moses was warned when he was about to build the tabernacle: "See to it that you make everything according to the pattern shown you on the mountain." But in fact the ministry Jesus has received is as superior to theirs as the covenant of which he is mediator is superior to the old one, since the new covenant is established on better promises. For if there had been nothing wrong with that first covenant, no place would have been sought for another. But God found fault with the people and said: the days are coming, declares the Lord, when I will make a new covenant with the people of Israel and with the people of Judah. It will not be like the covenant I made with their ancestors when I took them by the hand to lead them out of Egypt, because they did not remain faithful to my covenant, and I turned away from them, declares the Lord. This is the covenant I will establish with the people of Israel after that time, declares the Lord.

I will put my laws in their minds and write them on their hearts. I will be their God, and they will be my people. No longer will they teach their neighbor, or say to one another, 'Know the Lord, because they will all know me, from the least of them to the greatest. For I will forgive their wickedness and will remember their sins no more." By calling this covenant "new," he has made the first one obsolete; and what is obsolete and outdated will soon disappear.

Also Hebrews 9:15 says, "For this reason Christ is the mediator of a new covenant, that those who are called may receive the promised eternal inheritance—now that he has died as a ransom to set them free from the sins committed under the first covenant."

You see, Jesus is the High Priest of this new covenant which provides us unfiltered and direct access to him.

Hebrews 10:19–22 says, "**Therefore, brothers and sisters, since we have confidence to enter the Most Holy Place by the blood of Jesus**, by a new and living way opened for us through the curtain, that is, his body, and since we have a great priest over the house of God, **let us draw near to God** with a sincere heart and with the full assurance that faith brings, having our hearts sprinkled to cleanse us from a guilty conscience and having our bodies washed with pure water.

It is important to point out that with this new priesthood established by Jesus for this new covenant, comes a change of law and order. Hebrews 7:12 says, "For the priesthood being changed, of necessity there is also a change in the law."

Question: What was the change in the law and order?

PART 2: THE BOOK OF HEBREWS

What exactly changed? It's obvious I want to point out that tithing requirements changed. I will elaborate more on this change later in this chapter, but before we address tithing in the New Testament, it's imperative I provide you with an overview of the Book of Hebrews. You may question "Why do I need an overview of the Book of Hebrews?" Well the answer is simple, because the **only** time tithing is mentioned in the New Testament is in this book - Hebrews Chapter 7.

We've already established the New Testament officially began after the death of Jesus. Did you know from the time of Jesus' death until the end of the book of Revelations there is absolutely no mention of the word "tithe" aside from Hebrews Chapter 7? If you don't believe me, prove me wrong, check for yourself.

Given this chapter is the **only** chapter in the New Testament that mentions tithes, I am calling this chapter, "The Great Debate." However, before we address The Great Debate (Hebrews 7), first I will provide you with an overview of the Book of Hebrews. This initial overview is critical in establishing a foundational understanding of the writer's intent for writing this book, along with providing us with the proper context we should interpret in Hebrews.

Let's begin.

An "unknown" writer wrote the book of Hebrews. Though there has been a lot of speculation about who wrote this book, some suggest possibly Apollos, Barnabas or even Paul may have authored this book. Regardless to who penned this letter we know this letter was written to Jewish-Christians who were being persecuted for believing in Christ. To escape the persecution these Jewish-Christians were considering returning to Judaism - the Jewish system of the law. The unknown writer was encouraging them to persevere in the face of this persecution. He endeavored to reassure them that believing in Christ as Savior was no mistake. The overall theme of Hebrews can be found in the word "BETTER". The writer wanted these Jewish-Christians to fully embrace Jesus as Savior knowing what they have in him is far BETTER than Judaism.

In Jesus they have:

* Better Revelation [1:1,2]
* Better Expectation [6:9]
* Better Hope [7:19]
* Better Priesthood [7:7-11; 20-28]
* Better Testament (covenant) [7:22; 8:6]
* Better Promises [8:6]
* Better Sacrifices [8:6]
* Better Possessions [10:34]
* Better Country [11:16]
* Better Resurrection [11:35]

In his *performance*, Jesus provides a "Better":

* Better Priesthood
* Better Sanctuary
* Better Covenant
* Better Sacrifice

In his *person*, Jesus is "Better" than:

* The Angels
* Moses
* Joshua
* Abraham

Understanding the theme **better** is essential for us addressing The Great Debate – in Hebrews Chapter 7. It's also important for you to know the Jews in Judaism held Angels, Moses, Joshua and Abraham in high-esteem. In order to persuade these Jewish-Christians to fully embrace Christ they would have to convince them that Jesus is better/superior than each of these four: Angels, Moses, Joshua and Abraham. Having this foundational understanding will help tremendously in putting Hebrews Chapter 7 into proper prospective.

* Better than the Angels – Hebrews "Chapter" 1
* Better than Moses – Hebrews 3
* Better than Joshua – Hebrews 4
* Better than Abraham – Hebrews 7

PART 3: THE GREAT DEBATE – ABRAHAM'S TITHE PT. 2 (HEBREWS 7)

It bears repeating that tithing is only mentioned in one single chapter in the **entire** New Testament. That's some kind of emphasis, huh? Not very much at all. Teachers generally avoid using this chapter to teach tithing, but whenever they do, it's common to hear verses out of context. I'll explain what I mean more in detail later in this chapter.

After I studied this book in its entirety, I realized what the heart of the writer's message was when he wrote this chapter. Against the belief of some, I can assure you that this chapter is not teaching or endorsing tithing in the New Testament. This chapter centers on two primary insights:

1) Melchizedek is superior to Abraham, therefore since Jesus became a high priest after the order of Melchizedek, he too is superior to Abraham and the Levitical priesthood.
2) Jesus is undoubtedly qualified to be High Priest.

Those two insights perfectly summarizes this chapter, now please allow me to build my case. If you noticed leading up to Hebrews 7 the writer was attempting to explain in both chapters 5 and 6 that Jesus was qualified to be High Priest. It's crucial you understand why this statement was extremely troubling to these Jewish-Christians. Although they believed in Christianity they still took pride in their religious culture and heritage, much of their persecution was directly related to them going against their religious culture and heritage, practicing Christianity over Judaism. In Christianity they would have to go against Judaism and accept Jesus replacing the Levitical Priesthood. Due to the extreme persecution related to Jesus replacing the Levitical priesthood, some were tempted to revert back to Judaism. However, the writer exhorts them to persevere.

Here is an assignment before we move onto the next chapter. I'd like you to pick up your bible and read Chapters 5 & 6 of Hebrews. When you're done, pick back up here at this point.

Now that you're done reading both chapters, I'd like to ask you a question. Based upon what you've read, what is the *main point* the writer is attempting to make?

Put your answer here: _____

Perhaps you nailed it with the correct answer, let's find out. The correct answer to this question can be found in the very last verse of chapter 6. Hebrews 6:20 says, "<u>Where the forunner has entered for us, even Jesus, having become High Priest forever according to the order of Melchizedek</u>." The main point the writer was making centered on the claim that Jesus is undoubtedly qualified to be our high priest according to the order of Melchizedek, whereas now in chapter 7 his sole purpose is PROVING that claim.

Hebrews 7 is not a teaching on tithing or a command to tithe. It's a chapter that proves Jesus is undoubtedly qualified to be our High Priest.

I call this chapter The Great Debate, because some that teach New Testament tithing contend this chapter supports it, however, once this chapter is understood and interpreted in its proper context, it'll be plain to see it's no endorsement on New Testament tithing. Despite me calling this chapter, The Great Debate, by no means do I believe this chapter is debatable, especially once you understand the gist of this chapter.

There is truly no debate regarding the key focus of the writer to these Jewish-Christians. If I were to paraphrase the writer's key point of this chapter, I'd say, "Jesus is qualified to be our High Priest forever according to the order of Melchizedek."

In order to fully appreciate and understand this chapter, it's critical you understand the significance of this statement directed to these Jewish-Christians. The idea of Jesus being our high priest according to the order of Melchizedek was quite disturbing. It was disturbing because the Jews knew *all* priests were required to come from the **Tribe of Levi** – without exception. The issue here is Jesus was from the wrong tribe - **Tribe of Judah.** The Jewish-Christian knew that alone would disqualify him from the priesthood.

In the light of this dilemma, the writer smoothly segues into this chapter in an effort to prove Jesus is undoubtedly qualified to be high priest, despite being from the wrong tribe. In this chapter the writer intends to prove (1) Melchizedek's order was superior to the Levitical order and (2) Jesus is qualified to be our High Priest. This is the proper perspective to study this chapter from. **Nowhere will you find a command to tithe**.

In an effort to simplify this chapter, I've broken it down into three parts:

Part 1: Superiority of Melchizedek [Hebrews 7:1-10]

a. Melchizedek was a Priest and a King. [1]
b. Melchizedek is a **type** of Christ, not **actually** him. [3]
c. Even Abraham acknowledged his superiority by receiving his blessing and tithed to him in response to his blessing. [4]
d. Verse 8 is not instructing us to tithe in the New Testament. The Great Debate really centers on this 8th verse. Some teachers of New Testament tithing suggest heavily that this verse substantiates the belief that we should continue tithing like Abraham in the New Testament, except to Jesus. They teach verse 8 is referring to Jesus, however that is not true, verse 8 is actually referring to **Melchizedek**.

If we are to tithe in the New Testament based upon verse 8, then we would need to tithe to Melchizedek.

From the amplified translation, I want you to look at Hebrews 7:8–10:

(8) Furthermore, here [in the Levitical priesthood] tithes are received by men who are subject to death; while there [in the case of Melchizedek], they are received by one of whom it is testified that he lives [perpetually].

(9) A person might even say that Levi [the father of the priestly tribe] himself, who received tithes, paid tithes through Abraham [the father of all Israel and of all who believe],

(10) For Levi was still in the loins (unborn) of his forefather [Abraham] when Melchizedek met him (Abraham).

The word 'resemble' means to be like or similar to. No one would argue the fact that kids resemble their biological parents, yet they are not *actually* their parents.

> "Melchizedek *resembled* Christ, but he was not *actually* Christ"

Verse 8 essentially was intended to compare both priesthoods and point out the superiority of the Melchizedek priesthood over the Levitical priesthood. In verse 9 it says, "A person might even say that Levi [the father of the priestly tribe] himself, who received tithes, paid tithes through Abraham [the father of all Israel and of all who believe]. This verse indicates Levi [the father of the priestly tribe] **theoretically** tithe to Melchizedek through Abraham. The implication is that even Levi [the father of the priestly tribe] acknowledged the superiority of Melchizedek by theoretically tithing through Abraham. It's imperative to point out what this theory entails. In Eastern society thought, it is believed whatever your ancestors did – you did. A prime example of this thought-process would be the bible indicating because Adam [the father of humanity] sinned – all of humanity sinned. Needless to say you and I didn't physically partake of the sinful forbidden fruit, however in theory [Eastern thought], we did.

Now that you understand these verses in light of its true meaning and proper context, we can summarize them by saying Melchizedek was *so superior* that not only did Abraham tithe to him, but also Levi [the father of the priestly tribe] did as well.

Note: **The tithe was *only* mentioned here to establish the superiority of Melchizedek**. The proof of that can be found in Heb. 7:7 when it says the less [referring to Abraham] is blessed by the greater [referring to Melchizedek]. <u>Therefore, if anyone suggests you tithe based upon Heb. 7: 8, you'd have to tithe to Melchizedek because that's who verse 8 is referring to – not Jesus.</u>

Along with this new priesthood comes a new law according to Heb. 7:12 "For the priesthood being change, of necessity there be a change of the law." The burden of proof for those teaching New Testament tithing would be to show under this new law the Law of Christ, we should tithe.

Do we tithe under the Law of Christ? Based upon the Apostles teachings of Christ, there is absolutely **no** supporting evidence of tithing being a requirement under this law. None of the Apostles required tithes, demonstrated tithing or even mentioned tithing, particularly the Apostle Paul who was an incredibly strict follower of the law prior to his conversion to Christianity.

Question: If tithing was a requirement for the New Testament church, wouldn't it be strange that Paul didn't teach the Gentile Christians that principle? 1 Timothy 2:7 says, "Whereunto I am ordained a preacher, and an apostle, (I speak the truth in Christ, *and* lie not;) a teacher of the Gentiles in faith and verity." Paul indicates here he was called to teach the Gentiles the message of faith and verity. So what is faith and verity? Faith is a system of religious beliefs, whereas verity is something that is true, as a principle belief, idea, or statement. *Given the Gentile-Christians were not taught the customs and practices of Judaism, they would understandably be unfamiliar with tithing. Also, they would have needed to be taught tithing if it was a requirement. In not one of Paul's epistles (letters to the church) did he mention tithing to the Gentiles.*

Given this insight, tithing couldn't have been required because it was never mentioned by the Apostle Paul or any other apostle. However you don't have to take my word for it, search the scriptures yourself, or better yet, ask those who teach tithing to provide you their New Testament references.

Part II: Need for a New Priesthood. [Hebrews 7:11-22]

a. The writer continues to emphasize the inferiority and weakness of the Levitical priesthood and law. The writer also describes that God offered us something better through Christ. [11, 18,19]
b. Verse 15 re-emphasizes that Melchizedek was ***not actually*** Christ, rather **like** him. [15]
c. Even though Christ was from the wrong tribe, he's undeniably qualified to be priest. [13-22]

Part III: The writer ends his case – Case Closed! [Hebrews 7:20-28]

The writer reinforces his point that Jesus is undeniably qualified, better and the final High Priest.

a. By Qualified: He's wants them to know Jesus is sealed and approved. [Hebrews 7:20-21]
b. By Better: He wanted these Jewish-Christians to understand and accept the fact that our new priesthood is far better than the old priesthood. In verse 22 he says Jesus is our surety for this new covenant. Meaning he takes full responsibility for its performance. [Hebrews 7:22]

c. The Final High Priest:
   I really want you to get this point. The last part of this chapter ends the exact opposite from how the chapter begins. The beginning of this chapter portrayed the *weakness* of the priesthood due to their subjection to death, however the last part of this chapter depicts the *strength* of this new covenant because Jesus our High Priest lives forevermore! [Hebrews 7:23-28]

Abraham tithed according to Hebrews 7

Hopefully after reading this breakdown of this chapter you have a full grasp of what this chapter is primarily about. I've attempted to debunk the erroneous teaching I've heard related to this chapter. In case you're still on the bubble to whether Abraham's example of tithing transcends into the New Testament, I will provide you will further insight into the Abrahamic tithe account.

Hebrews 7 is simply a description of Abraham tithing, not a *command* for us to tithe. As you learned, tithing was only mentioned to substantiate the superiority of Melchizedek over the Levitical priesthood. There's no place where you'll find a single command to tithe or a command to follow Abraham's example of tithing. Just because Abraham tithed in Genesis before the law doesn't imply tithing transcends into the New Testament.

Let's re-examine Abraham's Tithing Account:

Insight #1: Abraham practiced circumcision before the Law, but that doesn't mean we should adopt that practice? [Genesis 17:10-14]

Also in Genesis 22 Abraham was about to offer his son Isaac as a sacrifice to God. I don't see anyone following this Abrahamic practice. My point is just because Abraham did something during his walk with God doesn't necessarily apply to the New Testament church, unless we're otherwise commanded to through by the apostolic teachings.

Insight #2: Abraham's tithe was not a requirement, rather a "voluntary act." It was a gift to Melchizedek in response to his blessing. [Genesis 14:18-20]

Genesis 14:18-24, "Then Melchizedek king of Salem brought out bread and wine. He was priest of God Most High, and he blessed Abram, saying, "Blessed be Abram by God Most High, Creator of heaven and earth. And praise be to God Most High, who delivered your enemies into your hand." Then Abram gave him a tenth of everything. The king of Sodom said to Abram, "Give me the people and keep the goods for yourself." But Abram said to the king of Sodom, "With raised hand I have sworn an oath to the Lord, God Most High, Creator of heaven and earth, that I will accept nothing belonging to you, not even a thread or the strap of a sandal, so that you will never be able to say,

I made Abram rich. I will accept nothing but what my men have eaten and the share that belongs to the men who went with me—to Aner, Eshkol and Mamre. Let them have their share."

It's important again to point out Abraham not only gave the tithe, the tenth, of the spoils away, but he gave it *all* away. He gave the tenth tithe to Melchizedek and the remainder to the King of Sodom, minus what his soldiers ate. *So essentially if we're building practices solely off this specific example we would need to give **all** our money away, not just the tithe – the tenth, because* Abraham gave it ALL away.

Insight #3: Here's more proof Abraham's tithe was a *voluntary act, not a requirement*. According to Genesis 13:2 Abraham was a rich man, but there's absolutely **no proof of him ever tithing on a regular basis. There is proof of him *not* tithing on a regular basis**.

In Genesis a man by the name of Abimelech blessed Abraham with livestock and money and Abraham did not tithe. Genesis 20:14-17 says, "And Abimelech took sheep, and oxen, and menservants, and womenservants, and gave them unto Abraham, and restored him Sarah his wife. And Abimelech said, Behold, my land is before thee: dwell where it pleaseth thee. *And unto Sarah he said, Behold, I have given thy brother a thousand pieces of silver: behold, he is to thee a covering of the eyes, unto all that are with thee, and with all other: thus she was reproved.* So Abraham prayed unto God: and God healed

Abimelech, and his wife, and his maidservants; and they bare children."

Now if tithing was a requirement commanded by God, such as circumcision, why didn't Abraham tithe on this occasion after receiving livestock and money? *He didn't, therefore we must conclude tithing wasn't his regular practice or a direct command from God.*

> *"There is no proof Abraham **did tithe** on a regular basis, however there is proof he **did not tithe** on a regular basis."*

Lastly, in the New Testament when describing what we should glean from Abraham's life, it never suggests we follow his physical walk with God, rather his spiritual (faith) walk with God. Abraham is acclaimed as the father of faith. It's his example of faith in God's promises we are encouraged to follow. Therefore we aren't expected to lay our sons on the altar like he did in his physical walk with God. God simply expects us to emulate the faith he exhibited when he laid his son on the altar as a sacrifice. Romans 4:12 says, "And the father of circumcision to them who are not of the circumcision only, but who also **walk in the steps of that faith of our father Abraham**, which *he had* being *yet* uncircumcised."

> *"It's not Abraham's physical walk with God we're to follow, rather his spiritual (faith) walk."*

Though his physical lifestyle was flawed, his lifestyle of faith was excellent! Therefore we're not to follow his physical walk, because it was faulty. Abraham made several poor decisions like most people following God. He lied to the King about Sarah not being his wife. He also slept with Hagar and had Ishmael which wasn't apart of God's plan. I'm not dragging Abraham for his imperfection, but it's obvious his physical walk with God was far from perfect. Although Abraham exhibited weakness in his physical walk with God, he provided a great example of strong faith in God's promises. Romans 4:18-22 says, "Who against hope believed in hope, that he might become the father of many nations, according to that which was spoken, so shall thy seed be. And being not weak in faith, he considered not his own body now dead, when he was about an hundred years old, neither yet the deadness of Sara's womb: He staggered not at the promise of God through unbelief; but was *strong in faith*, giving glory to God; And being fully persuaded that, what he had promised, he was able also to perform. And therefore it was imputed to him for righteousness."

Abraham provides the best example that despite our individual physical weaknesses and mistakes, if you have faith in God's promises, you can still be victorious.

Hebrews 11:8-19 says, "By faith Abraham, when called to go to a place he would later receive as his inheritance, obeyed and went, even though he did not know where he was going. By faith he made his home in the promised-land like a stranger in a foreign country; he lived in tents, as did Isaac and Jacob, who were heirs with him of the same promise. For he was looking forward to the city with foundations, whose architect and builder is God. And by faith even Sarah, who was past childbearing age, was enabled to bear children because she considered him faithful who had made the promise. And so from this one man, and he as good as dead, came descendants as numerous as the stars in the sky and as countless as the sand on the seashore. All these people were still living by faith when they died. They did not receive the things promised; they only saw them and welcomed them from a distance, admitting that they were foreigners and strangers on earth. People who say such things show that they are looking for a country of their own. If they had been thinking of the country they had left, they would have had opportunity to return. Instead, they were longing for a better country—a heavenly one. Therefore God is not ashamed to be called their God, for he has prepared a city for them. By faith Abraham, when God tested him, offered Isaac as a sacrifice. He who had embraced the promises was about to sacrifice his one and only son, even though God had said to him, "It is through Isaac that your offspring will be reckoned." Abraham reasoned that God could even raise the dead, and so in a manner of speaking he did receive Isaac back from death."

God desires to be believed! *"But without faith it is impossible to please him, for he who comes to God must believe that he is, and that he is a rewarder of those who diligently seek him."* *[Hebrews 11:6]*

Abraham exhibited this faith in God and that's why he gave the tithe and the remainder of the spoil away. He esteemed the spiritual blessing from Melchizedek greater than the possessions [Genesis 14:18-20]; and he gave the remainder of the spoil to King of Sodom because he didn't want anyone to take credit for the manifestation he believed he would receive by faith.

Following this act of faith of giving all the spoils away, immediately God told Abraham in Genesis 15:1, "I am your shield, your exceeding great reward!"

Some would say Abraham's unusual giving was an act of gratitude, for God helping him supernaturally defeat four King's Armies with only three-hundred and eighteen trained servants. Reference: Genesis 14:14

Do I believe this was an act of Abraham's gratitude? Yes, I do agree it was an act of gratitude, but what is gratitude if it's forced? I believe it wasn't forced, rather voluntary. That's what makes his act so significant to God. We should also mirror this attitude of gratitude Abraham exhibited and give to God for all the victories we've won. This giving should be done without bullying, coercion and compulsion. It should require no certain amount or percentage. It should be a token of your appreciation for the victories He's given you. The point is, God isn't concerned with the size of your giving. He's concerned with the size of the heart giving it.

That's the New Testament kind of giving!

Chapter 6

APOSTLE PAUL ON TITHING AND GIVING

PART 1: NEW TESTAMENT GIVING

Congrats, you've made it to the final part of our study! I'm really excited about this Chapter because I can finally reveal the New Testament way of giving. I'm sure there are some who initially read the title of this book and immediately thought this was a book about not giving to the church. Hopefully after reading this chapter, it will be realized that tithing under the New Covenant is completely wrong. This book isn't intended to be a tool to support anti-Christians' agendas to discredit the church. Nor is this book an attempt to stop or slow down people from financially contributing to the church. This book is essentially about explaining the true way God intends for Christians to give in the New Testament.

Per my allegory example in the introduction – this book is about Truth exposing Lie – erroneous teaching. I want to be perfectly clear, I don't believe the majority of those teaching tithing are aware of their error, however that doesn't negate the fact the message is erroneous.

Hopefully I have provided you with sufficient information that leads you to realize that tithing doesn't apply to the church today. I hope learning this truth has set you free in your soul. When I say soul, I mean your mind, will, and emotions. Now that you realize God isn't mad at you, you're no thief, and you're not cursed with a curse you should be free from any negative feelings related to not tithing. In Jesus we're blessed, not cursed, because he has freed us from the curse of the Law. Galatians 3:13 says, "Christ hath redeemed us from the curse of the law, being made a curse for us: for it is written, Cursed is every one that hangeth on a tree." Jesus paid the price for us on the cross, and now because of his BLOOD we're free from working to get God's approval. It's from this position of understanding we should give from an appreciation and gratitude for what He has done for us.

Nevertheless, the object of this Chapter is essentially to share the New Testament way of giving. This is where you will clearly see this book wasn't an attempt to stop or slow down your contributions to the church, rather it's about instructing you on the proper way of giving both inside and outside the church.

If there is a question about New Testament doctrine of giving, there's no person more qualified to help us understand than the Apostle Paul. The Apostle Paul is noted for writing over two-thirds of the New Testament. It's fair to say that if we cannot trust the Apostle Paul's teaching on giving, then we must question our salvation because Paul wrote the Book of Romans. You know Roman 9:9-10 is what you believe and confess to get saved, "That if thou shalt confess with thy mouth the Lord Jesus, and shalt believe in thine heart that God hath raised him from the dead, thou shalt be saved. For with the heart man believeth unto righteousness; and with the mouth **confession is made unto salvation**."

Paul was never timid about his apostolic authority. He made it very clear his message was from Jesus, not man! Paul says in Galatians 1: 6-14, "I marvel that ye are so soon removed from him that called you into the grace of Christ unto another gospel. Which is not another; but there be some that trouble you, and would pervert the gospel of Christ. But though we, or an angel from heaven, preach any other gospel unto you than that which we have preached unto you, let him be accursed. As we said before, so say I now again, if any man preach any other gospel unto you than that ye have received, let him be accursed. For do I now persuade men, or God? Or do I seek to please men? For if I yet pleased men, I should not be the servant of Christ. But I certify you, brethren that the gospel which was preached of me is not after man. For I neither received it of man, neither was I taught it, but by the revelation of Jesus Christ. For ye have heard of my conversation in time past in the Jews' religion, how that beyond measure I persecuted the church of God, and wasted it; And profited in the Jews' religion above many my equals in mine own nation, being more exceedingly zealous of the traditions of my fathers."

Did Paul ever teach tithing as part of the gospel message? No, so why have we taught and accepted this principle of tithing as part of the gospel? Paul's teachings should be trusted as God's message to the church. Paul states in 2 Timothy 3:14-16 AMP, "But continue thou in the things which thou hast learned and hast been assured of, knowing of whom thou hast learned them; And that from a child thou hast known the holy scriptures, which are able to make thee wise unto salvation through faith which is in Christ Jesus. **All scripture is given by inspiration of God, and is profitable for doctrine, for reproof, for correction, for instruction in righteousness**: That the man of God may be perfect, thoroughly furnished unto all good works."

According to 2 Timothy 3:16 the Word of God should be our final authority on doctrinal matters. That's essentially what this study is about, correcting erroneous teaching on tithing and providing the correct instructions on New Testament giving.

Here are (5) points we'll be covering on New Testament giving:

1) Should we give to the church? Does giving outside the church matter to God?
2) Should preachers get paid? If so, how much?
3) Since we aren't required to tithe, how much should we give?
4) What should be our motivation for giving? When should we give?
5) Is there corruption in the church related to the Prosperity Message?

SHOULD WE GIVE TO THE CHURCH? DOES GIVING OUTSIDE THE CHURCH MATTER TO GOD?

First off, let me say whatever source(s) you receive the Word from you have a responsibility to provide that source your financial support. For instance, if you receive the Word primarily from your local church, you have a biblical responsibility to financially support that church. Galatians 6:6 says, "Let him who receives instructions in the Word [of God] share all good things with his teacher [contributing to his support]." This principle is applicable to both regular and irregular church visitation. You have a responsibility to contribute to that source even if your visits are irregular.

As it relates to giving to the church, it's very clear God expects us to be financial contributors to the church. Paul says in 1 Corinthians 16:1-2 AMP, "<u>Now concerning the *money* collected for [the relief of] the saints [in Jerusalem], you are to *do the same as I **directed the churches** of Galatia to do*. On the first day of every week each one of you is to put something aside, in **proportion to his prosperity**, and save it so that no collections [will need to] be made when I come.</u>"

Here we have our answer to whether or not we should give to the church? Based upon this passage, we absolutely should! Also you see **what** we should give - money, not time. Giving your time to the church definitely has its place, but it's no substitute for the church collection. Paul directed the saints in both churches, Galatia and Corinth, to give therefore I surmise this is one demonstration of New Testament giving. *It's important to note Paul never requested a specific amount or tithe, rather he said every man should give in* **proportion to his prosperity**. I call this type of giving "**commensurable giving**."

Did you notice the principle here that I've emphasized numerous of times? "What God prescribes (commands), he describes (provide instructions)."

Prescribes (Command)	Describes (Instructs)
1 Corinthians 16:1	1 Corinthians 16:2
Now concerning the *money* collected for [the relief of] the saints [in Jerusalem], you are to do the same as I directed the churches of Galatia to do.	On the first day of every week each one of you is to put something aside, in proportion to his prosperity, and save it so that no collections [will need to] be made when I come.

Does giving outside the church matter to God?

I'm frequently asked the question, does giving outside the church matter to God? This is asked by people with big hearts who desire to give to organizations and individuals outside the church. These people oftentimes are very passionate about helping the less fortunate. They very often prefer to take some of their church money and give it towards a cause they're deeply passionate about.

Most of these people have great concerns about what, where and how their church contributions are used. These concerns are highly attributed to the lack of financial transparency within the church. If you share this sentiment, let me tell you, you're not being irrational. Churches aren't perfect, even if you or I led them, so let's be fair. This is certainly one area I believe most churches can improve upon. I believe people would be far more motivated to give, if they were aware of how the money collected was helping hurting people. Yes, people need the church's spiritual help, however physical help shouldn't go ignored. James 2:14-16 NKJV says, "What does it profit my brethren, if someone says he has faith but does not have works? Can faith save him? If a brother or sister is naked and destitute of daily food, and one of you say to them, "Depart in peace, be warmed and filled," but you do not give them the things are needed for the body, what does it profit?"

We have a duty to give outside the church in order to meet the physical needs of our fellow man. There are multiple ways to give outside the church and I find it hard to believe that God is opposed to us doing so.

For example, I'm a St. Jude supporter! I'm passionate about this organization because I witnessed cancer eat my mother away until she died. After witnessing her succumb to this terrible disease, I couldn't imagine a kid going through this suffering. I'm compelled to help fight against this deadly disease. If you don't know, St. Jude's is a hospital for research and treatment for children with cancer or other life-threatening diseases. The part I love is no family receives a bill, it's all free! St. Jude provides me that avenue to help fight against this terrible disease. This organization and others like it need our financial contributions and I have been a proud supporter for many years.

This is just one of the many organizations that focuses on helping the disadvantaged. However, many of us don't have to look very far, there are people right within our social circles that need our help such as family, friends and neighbors. The Good Samaritan story is a perfect example of how we should seek to help people that cannot help themselves outside the church.

Luke 10:30-37, "In reply Jesus said: "A man was going down from Jerusalem to Jericho, when he was attacked by robbers. They stripped him of his clothes, beat him and went away, leaving him half dead. A priest happened to be going down the same road, and when he saw the man, he passed by on the other side. So too, a Levite, when he came to the place and saw him, passed by on the other side. But a Samaritan, as he traveled, came where the man was; and when he saw him, he took pity on him. He went to him and bandaged his wounds, pouring on oil and wine. Then he put the man on his own donkey, brought him to an inn and took care of him. The next day he took out two denarii and gave them to the innkeeper. 'Look after him,' he said, 'and when I return, I will reimburse you for any extra expense you may have. "Which of these three do you think was a neighbor to the man who fell into the hands of robbers?" The expert in the law replied, "The one who had mercy on him." Jesus told him, "Go and do likewise."

God does expect us to give outside the church...

Unfortunately, many churches are guilty of not emphasizing this form of giving or even teaching it at all. Most churches expect their members to give exclusively to them. While it's important to give to our local churches, it's equally important to help others outside the church such as we saw in the Good Samaritan story. This topic is interesting because I've noticed people tend to be on either side of the spectrum. Some people either give all their money to the church, while others opt to give all their money outside of the church. We are to give to the church, yet we also should be open and available to help those outside the church that need a hand-up, such as the Good Samaritan did.

The Apostle Paul states, "James, Cephas and John, those esteemed as pillars, gave me and Barnabas the right hand of fellowship when they recognized the grace given to me. They agreed that we should go to the Gentiles, and they to the circumcised. **All they asked was that we should continue to remember the poor, the very thing I had been eager to do all along.**" [Galatians 2:9-10]

While it is true the Apostles were greatly concerned with the church's spiritual and financial needs, you also see giving to the poor was of great concern as well. The circumcised depicts "saved" people inside the church, whereas Gentile depicts "unsaved" people outside the church. This passage makes it clear we should help people outside the church.

Let's consider this question. What comes to mind when you think about the poor? Most people immediately think of a homeless person or a panhandler. Going forward when you think of the poor, let's not limit this to a homeless person or a panhandler begging on the side of the road. Actually, the true poor is someone that needs a *hand-up* in life. A hand-up, not so much a one-time hand-out.

"The true poor needs a hand-up not a hand-out"

The true poor can be a widow on a fixed income. The true poor can be a fatherless kid. The true poor can be an underemployed single mother or father. The true poor can be a person that has recently loss their job. The true poor can be someone with a physical disability that prevents them from gainful employment. In this economy the true poor can also be the struggling middle income person living a hand-to-mouth existence, they're considered the working poor. If they find themselves in a crunch, they make too much money to get assistance from the government and oftentimes the church as well. Most people ignore this group, but it's a fact you can work and budget well and still need a hand-up from time to time in this economy. I know this list isn't exhausted, there are many other examples of people that are truly poor. By true poor I mean people that need a **HAND-UP,** not a one-time hand-out. I believe God wants to move upon our hearts to help these individuals.

What Paul exhorts rich Christians to do in 1 Timothy 6:17-18 says, "Charge them that are rich in this world, that they be not high-minded, nor trust in uncertain riches, but in the living God, who giveth us richly all things to enjoy; That they do good, that they be rich in good works, ready to distribute, willing to communicate."

Paul said the rich should be rich in good works, distributing and giving! The level of giving should be consistent with your level of prosperity – remember we call this *Commensurable Giving.*

> *"Our giving should be consistent with our level of prosperity"*

God never intended for us to be rich so we can be selfish and flaunt our wealth in front of those who are less fortunate. He intended for those with more resources to be more resourceful. To whom much is given much is required. It has been my observation that some Christians only aspire to be rich in an effort to accumulate a lot of material possessions and selfishly flaunt it like worldly people do. But as I stated, within the bible it says the rich should be rich in distributing to the needs of others less fortunate. *Please understand you can be earthly rich and heavenly poor, in the eyes of God.* Revelations 3:17 says, "Because thou sayest, I am rich, and increased with goods, and have need of nothing; and knowest not that thou art wretched, and miserable, and poor, and blind, and naked."

While I encourage us to help people and organizations outside of the church, I believe those who are in the family of Christ should eagerly seek opportunities to help each other. The bible tells us in Galatians 6:10, "As we have therefore opportunity, let us do good unto all men, <u>*especially* unto them who are of the household of faith</u>." The church is described as a "Household" meaning it should be a family-oriented community, a community that helps each other from within. Essentially we should seek to support each other, wherefore the money can circulate within our communities. It's nothing new, many groups practice this principle of money circulation. The Jewish community circulate their dollar eight times before it leaves their community. Interesting enough most churches help people outside of the church while neglecting those within. The bible says we should help "ALL" people, but *especially* those in the household of faith. Paul demonstrated this in Acts 20:35, "But now I go unto Jerusalem to minister unto the saints. For it hath pleased them of Macedonia and Achaia to make a certain contribution for the poor saints which are at Jerusalem."

The True Poor:

While it is true we should help the poor, we must not confuse the true poor with the needy. Paul said in Romans 15:26, "I have shewed you all things, how that so labouring ye ought to support the weak, and to remember the words of the Lord Jesus, how he said, It is more blessed to give than to receive." There is a difference between the true poor and the needy. The primary difference is the truly poor needs a hand-up to get into a better situation, while the needy wants only a hand-out to be comfortable in their current situation.

> *"The poor wants a hand-up, the needy wants a hand-out"*

Who the POOR is not:

1) The Lazy.

   Proverbs 6:10a says, "Yet a little sleep, a little slumber, a little folding of the hands to sleep: So shall thy poverty come as an armed man." Lazy people are not the true poor. They don't want a hand-up to help get on their feet, they'd rather take a hand-out to stay off their feet. Helping them only enables them to continue in their unproductive lifestyle.

2) People who make poor life choices.

Please note I'm not referring to people who have made past poor life decisions, repented and now need a hand-up. No, I'm referring to those that fail to change their self-destructive behavior. Proverbs 19:3 says, "The foolishness of man perverts his way: and his heart frets again God." These people deny any personal responsibility, rather they blame God, the system, family, and the dog for the consequences of their poor decisions. They fail to make better decisions to help themselves out of a bad situation. As the old saying goes, a drowning person must also participate in their rescue, if they're going to be saved. You shouldn't help these individuals until they've put forth true effort to help themselves. Ephesians 4:28 says, "Let him who stole steal no longer, but rather let him labor, working with his hands what is good, that he may have something to give him who has need." Paul exhorted these individuals to stop making poor choices that produce failure; they should begin making better decisions whereby they can be productive and help others.

3) The Busybodies and Disorderly.

2 Thessalonians 3:8-11 says, "Neither did we eat any man's bread for nought; but wrought with labour and travail night and day, that we might not be chargeable to any of you. Not because we have not power, but to make ourselves an ensample unto you to follow us. For even when we were with you, this we commanded you, that if any would not work, neither should he eat. For we hear that there are some which walk among you disorderly, working not at all, but are busybodies."

Busybodies are the individuals that make time for everything insignificant, but they can never quite find the time to do things that are beneficial to their progress. They are incredibly unproductive! While people are working, they're home watching reality T.V, playing video games, sleeping, surfing the web and of course posting on social media how great life is – oftentimes posting inspirational quotes. They're also frivolous spenders! They spend all their money on what they want, and beg for what they need.

The disorderly are Rebels! They play by their own rules, consequently they have an extremely difficult time holding down a job, because they don't like to play by the rules. They are not the true poor, Paul said these type of individuals need to suffer loss. Oftentimes, they have to hit rock bottom before they change. Helping them before that time unintentionally reinforces their poor behavior.

The poor isn't necessarily the needy!

Nevertheless God does desire us to help those that are genuinely in need of support, however we should be wise and avoid assisting those who take advantage of people's charitable hearts through manipulation. The true poor are those that if they could do better they would, they simply need a hand-up until then, however the needy are those that have no interest in a hand-up, rather a hand-out, so they can be comfortable with not changing.

Jesus said in Matthew 26:11, "The poor you will always have with you." These are some of the people he was referring to. Unfortunately, everyone can't be helped because most won't help themselves. They go through life seeking hand-outs from the government as well as the church. If you tried giving them a hand-up, such as a job, they're likely look at you like you are crazy. If you observed God interactions with mankind, you'll notice he wasn't moved by *need*, rather faith or genuine effort, so why should you be moved by need alone?

SHOULD PREACHERS GET PAID? IF SO, HOW MUCH?

This question is also one of my most frequently asked questions. The way people feel about this is probably the leading reason I believe some folk object to the church collecting money. Due to people failing to understand the biblical perspective on preachers' compensations, it has led many to form their own personal opinions. There are numerous opinions on this subject, however I've divided the prevalent ones into three groups.

"3" types of opinions:

Group 1: The church Apathetic:

The church apathetical person truly dislikes the church and God. They really can care less about anything the two offers. They're critical on everything pertaining to the church and God even if it's good. Deep down most are offended with God and the church, therefore they seek any opportunity to discredit them. This group believes preachers shouldn't be paid and they mock those that give to the church.

Group 2: The Spiritual person and the Infrequent church goer:

The *spiritual person* doesn't attend church regularly for various reasons, however the primary reason is because they don't agree with organized religion led by a man. Whereas the *infrequent church goer* floats from church to church, because while they do believe in organized religion, they distrust preachers, therefore it's difficult for them to commit to a church. Though both groups don't hold complete contempt for the church, they are very suspicious about the preacher's income and lifestyle. Their opinions on this matter often changes, it's heavily influenced by what others think, the preachers reputation, and the preachers overall message. For example when I say overall message, if the preachers' overall message is all about money-money-money, this will likely highly impact this group's opinion.

Group 3: The Religious church goer:

This person is in the church whenever the doors swing open, but their bibles are closed. They don't read for themselves, they simply hear and believe every word that comes across the pulpit from their preacher. Whatever the preacher says, "Thus says the Lord", they believe without question. This person will argue with you that their preacher deserves *whatever* compensation they believe the good Lord wants them to have, even if they go broke giving to the church to pay it.

Considering everyone is persuaded by their own opinion and certainly has a right to their opinions, I won't waste my time arguing personal views. Conversely, there is one thing that cannot be argued and that's the truth, in this part of the study I will simply share the facts.

So should preachers get paid? The answer is yes, they should get paid. As Paul says to the Church of Corinth: Who serves as a soldier at his own expense? Who plants a vineyard and does not eat its grapes? Who tends a flock and does not drink the milk? Do I say this merely on human authority? Doesn't the Law say the same thing? For it is written in the Law of Moses: "Do not muzzle an ox while it is treading out the grain." Is it about oxen that God is concerned? Surely he says this for us, doesn't he? Yes, this was written for us, because whoever plows and threshes should be able to do so in the hope of sharing in the harvest. If we have sown spiritual seed among you, is it too much if we reap a material harvest from you? If others have this right of support from you, shouldn't we have it all the more? But we did not use this right. On the contrary, we put up with anything rather than hinder the gospel of Christ. Don't you know that those who serve in the temple get their food from the temple, and that those who serve at the altar share in what is offered on the altar? <u>In the</u>

same way, <u>the Lord has commanded that those who preach the gospel should receive their living from the gospel</u>. [1 Corinthians 9:7-14]

1 Corinthians 9:14 NKJV says, "Even so hath the Lord ordained that they which preach the gospel should live of the gospel." This verse makes it very clear preachers should be compensated.

Paul also received an offering from the Church of Philippi. Philippians 4:15-16 says, "Moreover, as you Philippians know, in the early days of your acquaintance with the gospel, when I set out from Macedonia, not one church shared with me in the matter of giving and receiving, except you only; [16] for even when I was in Thessalonica, you sent me aid more than once when I was in need. **It's important to point out that Paul didn't receive or demand a tithe or offering from any of his churches, these were all "voluntary" offerings.** <u>We know this because Paul indicates no other church gave offerings to him</u>, he states in verse 15, "Moreover, as you Philippians know, in the early days of your acquaintance with the gospel, when I set out from Macedonia, **not one church shared with me in the matter of giving and receiving, except you only.**"

Time to think logically. If tithing was a church requirement, giving wouldn't have been optional for this church or the others churches, right?

I must re-emphasize that the New Testament doesn't instruct pastors to receive their compensation from tithes or any mandatory offering, rather it instructs them to receive their compensation from the voluntary offerings of the people they serve.

The pastoral position can be misused to take advantage of people. Pastors are exhorted to use their positions responsibly. They have the right to provide *giving opportunities* to the people they serve, however afterwards they should trust God to move upon the people's heart to give accordingly. Pastors shouldn't use their position irresponsibly to fleece the people through manipulative tactics for self-gain. Nor should fear tactics be used to coerce people into giving. It's very unfortunate we have a religious scam that has become all too common in churches today, where the preacher is using manipulative tactics to get people to give above their true ability.

For example: When a church guest speaker puts everyone on the spot and says, "God said, everyone needs to bring their best offering now to the altar." Some even go a step further and request large amounts they claim God told them to request. They then demand everyone to line up in the front of the church according to the size of their offering. Intimidation! This and other similar types of manipulative tactics are NOT from God. **Remember if you feel *pressured or bullied it* isn't God's leading, rather man**!

Never give under those circumstances. 2 Timothy 1:7 AMP says, "For God did not give us a spirit of timidity (of cowardice, of craven and cringing and fawning fear), but (he has given us a spirit) of power and of love and of calm and well-balanced mind and discipline and self-control."

This book is designed to empower you with knowledge, so going forward you'll be bold and say no to religious scam artist.

SO HOW MUCH PREACHERS SHOULD GET PAID?

Of course no one has the exact amount they should get paid because the bible doesn't specify, however it does provide some guiding principles that should be used in approaching this matter.

1) Not based on getting rich!

   1 Peter 5:2 AMP – Tend (nurture, guard, guide, and fold) the flock of God that is [your responsibility], not by coercion or constraint, but willingly; <u>not dishonorably motivated by the disadvantages and profits [belonging to the office], but eagerly and cheerfully.</u>

It is vital that preachers genuinely evaluate their motives for why they desire to be in leadership. They must be honest with themselves and ask is it because they want a name among the hotshots? Wherefore broadcasting on television, building state-of-the-art facilities, purchasing airplanes and encouraging people to join their church isn't truly motivated by a sincere passion for souls, rather a means to making themselves a name and getting rich. Let me say this on the record, "I believe wholeheartedly most church leaders began ministry sincere," I'm by no means indicating all preachers set out to get rich from preaching the gospel. Starting off it's very common for preachers to suffer financially preaching the gospel. However, I do believe once they've experienced the financial advantages of preaching the gospel, thereafter some do become motivated by self-gain. This often leads them to take slight or sometimes full advantage of gullible religious people through abuse and misuse of their positional authority in the church.

A classic example of an advantage is church **nepotism**. Nepotism is an advantage most commonly taken by church leaders, particularly pastors. Nepotism is someone using their positional power or influence to favor relatives or friends by giving them jobs they may not be the best fit for. It's not uncommon for pastors to provide special opportunities to their family and friends without any regard for others that may be more qualified. It's normal to desire to help those we love and respect and if they are qualified and can hold their weight, then they should be highly considered. However, how many times have you seen one of these people featured on a church program – only to realize they didn't have a lick of talent? When this happens, everyone kind of just sits there tight-lipped cringing until the disaster is over. When church leaders place unqualified people in position, this wreaks havoc into the congregation. People may not tell their leader they're offended, most will either mentally check-out, lose their zest for engagement, or simply leave the church all together.

2) It should be adequate.

> 1 Timothy 5:17 AMP - Let the elders who perform their leadership duties well are to be considered worthy of double honor [and of *adequate financial support*), especially those who work hard at preaching and teaching [the word of God concerning eternal salvation through Christ].

Serving people can be quite a demanding job, especially if it's done with excellence. It's impossible for any leader to provide quality service if they are working a full-time job.

Acts 6:2-4, "So the Twelve gathered all the disciples together and said, "It would not be right for us to neglect the ministry of the word of God in order to wait on tables. Brothers and sisters, choose seven men from among you who are known to be full of the Spirit and wisdom. We will turn this responsibility over to them and will give our attention to prayer and the ministry of the word."

3) Commensurable to their **quality of service** and **quantity of service**.

   1 Timothy 5:17 says, those that perform **well and work hard** should receive more compensation. I believe *well* depicts **quality of service** rendered. These are the preachers that truly spend time digging into the Word and honing in on their skills to reach people they serve. When they speak you know they are well prepared because they've spent time with Jesus. They deserve more! Next, I believe the phrase *work hard* depicts **quantity of service** rendered. It's a fact anything that's good will likely grow, so it's highly probable preachers that serve well will have a larger following and with that comes more work. This verse suggests they should receive more compensation for their level of responsibility.

Exactly how much preachers should get paid is not my job to say. However it's my spirit-filled opinion they shouldn't be the ones deciding their own compensation. Non-profit organizations should have an executive board, perhaps they should address this matter. This is greatly beneficial for the preacher(s) being compensated. This will keep them above reproach, the cloud of suspicion in the sight of man. Apostle Paul exhibited this principle when he received an offering from the Church of Corinth [2 Cor. 8:1-21]. Paul stated in verses 20 & 21, "Avoiding this, that no man should blame us in this abundance which is administered by us: Providing for honest things, not only in the sight of the Lord, but also in the sight of men."

HOW MUCH SHOULD WE GIVE?

I've made one point very clear throughout this study and that's the bible doesn't instruct the New Testament Christians to tithe, rather to give. I know some preachers will have some serious concerns about this message because they'd likely assume it will drastically reduce membership giving. I hope after reading this chapter you'll be convinced that's not necessarily true. Nevertheless it's definitely not the nature of God to invoke fear into peoples' heart to tithe. God doesn't address us through fear tactics or intimidation to coerce us into serving or giving to him. "For God hath not given us the spirit of fear; but of power, and of love, and of a sound mind." [2 Timothy 1:6]

Please understand I once tithed, the problem was, I struggled to tithe at times and I felt like I was disappointing God when I couldn't. Overtime this sense of failure caused me to attend church irregularly. Most teach we must tithe on ALL increase, for the average person, that's difficult to do. This is essentially why so many have given up on trying to please God. Religion has made it complicated.

Also as a result of irregularly tithing, I also lacked confidence in my prayer life. I found myself hiding from God in my conscience due to the guilt of believing I was robbing God. Imagine if you owed a relative money and couldn't pay them back, you'd likely dodge them at family functions or perhaps avoid going to the function all together. I want you to know I didn't stop tithing because I was struggling. I'm not in the business of lowering God's targets so I can hit them. No, the Spirit of God gave me this revelation of New Testament giving, and that tithing wasn't a requirement. Every single point I've made so far has a chapter and verse within the bible supporting it. This revelation I received lifted a burden off my shoulders, I realized God loved me despite my monetary gift, big or small.

So to my Leaders, please don't think your members are seeking to avoid giving if they discontinue tithing. People have a right to give from a free and cheerful heart in response to Gods' goodness, opposed to fear and intimidation of being cursed if they don't tithe. As a leader your job is to provide the vision and the opportunity to give to that vison. Allow the Spirit of God to move upon the hearts of the people to give accordingly. Have faith that if God gave you the vision, he'll provide the provision.

"Where there's a God VISION, there will be God PROVISION"

Having said that, now allow me to share the biblical principles that will help you determine how much you should give.

PART 2: FIVE PRINCIPLES OF NEW TESTAMENT GIVING

PRINCIPLE #1: GIVE IN PROPORTION TO HOW GOD HAS PROSPERED YOU.

1 Corinthians 16:2 says, "On the first day of each week, let each one *of you [personally]* **put aside something and save it up as he has prospered [in proportion to what he is given]**, so that no collections will need to be taken after I come."

Take note on how Paul instructed his church to give. It's very conspicuous in its absence, he didn't mention a certain amount, percentage or even tithing. No, he instructed them to **give in proportion to how they prospered, which is – commensurable giving**. Based upon this principle of giving, how much is given will vary from individual to individual and from family to family. There's truly no one that can tell you what that amount should be, this is between you and God. However you should always give from a *place of integrity*. What I mean by place of integrity, is that you are honestly trying to do the right thing in your heart. When you operate in integrity, even if you're wrong, God won't hold it against you.

Notice in Genesis 20:1-7, "And Abraham journeyed from there to the South, and dwelt between Kadesh and Shur, and stayed in Gerar. Now Abraham said of Sarah his wife, "She *is* my sister." And Abimelech king of Gerar sent and took Sarah. But God came to Abimelech in a dream by night, and said to him, "Indeed you *are* a dead man because of the woman whom you have taken, for she *is* a man's wife." But Abimelech had not come near her; and he said, "Lord, will You slay a righteous nation also? Did he not say to me, 'She *is* my sister'? And she, even she herself said, 'He *is* my brother.' In the **integrity of my heart** and innocence of my hands I have done this." And God said to him in a dream, "Yes, I know that you did this in the **integrity of your heart.** For I also withheld you from sinning against Me; therefore I did not let you touch her. Now therefore, restore the man's wife; for he *is* a prophet, and he will pray for you and you shall live. But if you do not restore *her*, know that you shall surely die, you and all who *are* yours."

Notice the king pleaded with God considering his mistake. In verse Genesis 20:5, "Said he not unto me, she *is* my sister? And she, even she herself said, He *is* my brother: in the *integrity of my heart* and innocency of my hands have I done this. He tells God his mistake was done innocently from the integrity of his heart. As a result in verse 6, "And God said unto him in a dream, Yea, I know that thou didst this in the *integrity of thy heart*; for I also withheld thee from sinning against me: therefore suffered I thee not to touch her." We see God didn't hold this sin against him, solely due to the *integrity in his heart*.

Let me show you another example of **Commensurable Giving.**

Acts 11:29-30 AMP

(29) So the disciples resolved to send relief, **each according to his ability [in proportion as he had prospered]**, to the brethren who lived in Judea.

(30) And so they did, sending [their contributions] to the elders by the hand of Barnabas and Saul.

Once again you can see this principle is solely based upon one's ability and not any required amount, percentage or tithe.

I want to share one last reference on this principle of commensurable giving. Here's a challenge, I want you to read the passage below and see if you can identify the principle.

1 Timothy 6:17-18 AMP

(17) As for the rich in this world, charge them not to be proud and arrogant and contemptuous of others, nor to set their hopes on uncertain riches, but on God, Who richly and ceaselessly provides us with everything for [our] enjoyment.

(18) [Charge them] to do good, to be rich in good works, to be liberal and generous of heart, ready to share [with others],

Did you notice the principle? If so, put your answer in below:

_____
_____
_____

Okay, let me tell you what you should have identified. Carefully notice Paul said in verse 18, "[Charge them] to do good, to be rich in good works, to be liberal and generous of heart, ready to share [with others]." The rich should be *rich* in good works, ready to distribute, willing to share with others in good works, to be liberal and generous of heart, ready to share with others. The observation I wanted you to identify is *the rich should be rich in giving*. You see the correlation? The *ability* of the rich in giving [in proportion their prosperity] should be demonstrated in their giving. God requires the rich to give richly.

PRINCIPLE #2: GIVE FROM YOUR HEART.

This principle is imperative to our study, because it distinguishes the very difference between the Old Testament tithing from New Testament giving. Here's what the Apostle Paul said to the Church of Corinth.

2 Corinthians 9:1-12 AMP, "Now it is unnecessary for me to write to you about the offering [that is to be made] for the saints [in Jerusalem]; ²for I know your eagerness [to promote this cause], and I have [proudly] boasted to the people of Macedonia about it, telling them that Achaia has been prepared since last year [for this contribution], and your enthusiasm has inspired the majority of them [to respond]. ³Still, I am sending the brothers [on to you], so that our pride in you may not be an empty boast in this case, and so that you may be prepared, just as I told them you would be; ⁴otherwise, if any Macedonians come with me and find you unprepared, we—to say nothing of yourselves—will be humiliated for being so confident. ⁵That

is why I thought it necessary to urge these brothers to go to you [before I come] and make arrangements in advance for this generous, previously promised gift of yours, **so that it would be ready, not as something extorted [or wrung out of you], but as a [voluntary and] generous gift.** ⁶Now [remember] this: he who sows sparingly will also reap sparingly, and he who sows generously [that blessings may come to others] will also reap generously [and be blessed]. ⁷Let each one give [thoughtfully and with purpose] just as he has decided in his heart, not grudgingly or under compulsion, for God loves a cheerful giver [and delights in the one whose heart is in his gift]. ⁸And God is able to make all grace [every favor and earthly blessing] come in abundance to you, so that you may always [under all circumstances, regardless of the need] have complete sufficiency in everything [being completely self-sufficient in Him], and have an abundance for every good work *and* act of charity. ⁹As it is written *and* forever remains written, "He [the benevolent and generous person] scattered abroad, he gave to the poor, His righteousness endures forever!" ¹⁰<u>Now He who provides seed for the sower and bread for food will provide and multiply your seed for sowing [that is, your resources] and increase the harvest of your righteousness [which shows itself in active goodness, kindness, and love]</u>. ¹¹You will be enriched in every way so that you may be generous, and this [generosity, administered] through us is producing thanksgiving to God [from those who benefit]. ¹²For the ministry of this service (offering) is not only supplying the needs of the saints (God's people), but is also overflowing through many expressions of thanksgiving to God.

I want you to focus your attention on what Paul states in the second part of verse 5, "So that it would be ready, not as something extorted [or wrung out of you], but as a [**voluntary** and] generous gift." In a nutshell Paul stated giving shouldn't be forced, rather voluntary, and it should come from the heart. The core of New Testament giving centers on this insight. God is more concerned with the condition of your heart, than the actual gift. Whereas in the Old Testament tithing was mandatory (involuntary), because it was the law. How you felt in your heart was irrelevant. The fact of the matter is we're no longer under the law, rather grace, so why continue to adhere to any parts of it.

Paul had this issue with the Church of Galatia practicing circumcision. Paul firmly addresses this issue in Galatians 5:1-4 Paul as he wrote, "Stand fast therefore in the liberty by which Christ has made us free, and do not be entangled again with a yoke of bondage. Indeed I, Paul, say to you that become circumcised, Christ will profit you nothing. *And I testify again to every man who becomes circumcised that he is a debtor to keep the whole law. You have become estranged from Christ, you who attempt to be justified by law; you have fallen from grace.*"

Paul described circumcision, which was required under the Mosaic Law, as a yoke of bondage. Tithing would also fall in that category, a yoke of bondage, because it too was required under the law. Lastly, Paul said if we're determined to follow the law we must follow it completely, nor partially. Likewise, if we partially follow the law, we forfeit God's gift of Grace Jesus died to make available for us.

Now re-read 2 Corinthians 9:6-7

(6) Now [remember] this: he who sows sparingly will also reap sparingly, and he who sows [b]generously [that blessings may come to others] will also reap [c]generously [and be blessed].

(7) <u>Let each one give [thoughtfully and with purpose] just as he has decided in his heart</u>, <u>not grudgingly or under compulsion</u>, for God loves a cheerful giver [and delights in the one whose heart is in his gift].

These two verses emphatically prove the fact that New Testament giving should be done from the heart. You can clearly see instructions given to us on how **not** to give - grudgingly or under compulsion. This means preachers pushing or coercing you into giving is completely unbiblical – it's outright wrong! Again, it is not God's will that his children be forced, bullied or manipulated into giving. God desires our giving to be done *cheerfully and freely from the heart*. When I say, "freely from the heart" I mean from a place of spiritual freedom. God desires us to give from a place of spiritual freedom, not bondage derived from fear of being cursed.

This can be proven, notice what it says in verse 7, "Let each one give [thoughtfully and with purpose] just as he has decided in his heart." This proves giving should be intentional and come freely from the heart.

Free and cheerful giving should be a byproduct of our gratitude when we remember all God has done. Giving is a visible expression of worship, it's a token of our appreciation for all the resources God has provided us. When we give freely and cheerfully from our hearts, God will provide us with more seeds to sow and give us a harvest on what we've sown. Verse 10 says, "**Now He who provides seed for the sower** and bread for food will provide and multiply your seed for sowing [that is, your resources] and increase the harvest of your righteousness [which shows itself in active goodness, kindness, and love]."

It's very critical to highlight verse 10 didn't say he provides **tithe to the tither**, *no, it says he provides* **seed to the sower**. Did you catch that insight? If not, please re-read verse 10.

The last statistic I've heard pertaining to regular church tithers in the church was less than 15%. I know there are many reasons why the mass majority of Christians don't tithe. I believe the leading reason stems from having little to no results. Why? Mainly because most are tithing sparingly, grudgingly and through compulsion. We learned little results occur when we give sparingly, we reap sparingly. We gain little to no results when we give grudgingly or from compulsion, honestly we're likely to reap nothing.

Some churches are guilty for using Malachi 3:10, "Bring ye all the tithes into the storehouse, that there may be meat in mine house, and prove me now herewith, saith the LORD of hosts, if I will not *open you the windows of heaven*, and pour you out a blessing, that *there shall* not *be room* enough *to receive it*." Since we already addressed this verse, I won't re-address it, however we know now this was under the Old Testament covenant. Due to the fact we have a new covenant with better promises we shouldn't resort to the Old Testament principles, unless we're clearly advised to from the New Testament teachings.

You cannot use the Old Testament principle of tithing as a substitute for New Testament principle on giving!

Hear me loud and clear, "There's absolutely no blessing in obligational giving, unless God compelled you to give, then you're obligated." However if man puts the obligation on you, God isn't glorified, because you were forced. 2 Corinthians 9:7 from the Standard Kings James Version says "**Every man according as he purposeth in his heart, *so let him give*;** not grudgingly, or of necessity: for God loveth a cheerful giver." Paul said we shouldn't give out of ***necessity***. Let's define what necessity means?

Necessity means:

1) An imperative requirement or need for something.

2) The principle according to which something must be so, by virtue either of logic or of natural law.

3) The state of or fact of something being necessary or indispensable.

We can conclude necessity means a requirement, obligation or necessary. The Apostle Paul who wrote more than half of the New Testament said we shouldn't give from obligation. Next, I want to share some common forms of what I call, *Obligational Giving*, which occurs in some churches today.

1) **Tithing**

   If giving to the church is done under obligation it is wrong. However "if" you decide to make a tenth your baseline offering, that's between you and God. There's nothing wrong with that, unless God is directing you to give more. Remember your offering as a general principle should be commensurable to your level of prosperity or be Spirit-led, because God may ask you to give above what you consider you can afford at times. I will discuss Spirit-led giving in more detail briefly.

2) **The Offering Hustle**

You may be questioning what is the Offering Hustle? The offering hustle is when the preacher collects the offering like an auctioneer. They're basically hustling the offering! You may have witnessed an offering hustle during a church service. They start off requesting a certain amount. For example, they say, "Can I get $200, okay $200 going once $200 going twice? Can I get $100, okay $100 going once, $100 going twice? Can I get $50? Come on y'all, this is for the Lawd. Hasn't he been good to you? If so, give him your best offering." This hustle continues until they have applied enough pressure on everyone to give. If you've experienced this and fell for it, unfortunately you were hustled! These preachers are manipulators and very dishonest. The bible clearly tells us not to give under these circumstances, please don't fall for this religious scam! Always keep in mind God never wants anyone to give through spiritual coercion, emotional manipulation or bullying tactics.

PRINCIPLE #3: HOW MUCH SHOULD WE GIVE?

Read this statement very carefully, "Give freely from your heart, but give *how much* God has impressed upon your heart to give." So far, we've discussed giving from our hearts, now it's imperative we discuss the second form of giving and that is ***Spirit-led giving***.

Let's take a look at an example of Spirit-led giving.

Acts 4:31-37 states, "[31]And when they had prayed, the place where they were assembled together was shaken; and they were all filled with the Holy Spirit, and they spoke the word of God with boldness. [32]Now the multitude of those who believed were of one heart and one soul; neither did anyone say that any of the things he possessed was his own, but they had all things in common. [33]And with great power the apostles gave witness to the resurrection of the Lord Jesus. And great grace was upon them all. [34]Nor was there anyone among them who lacked; for all who were possessors of lands or houses sold them, and brought the proceeds of the things that were sold, [35]and laid *them* at the apostles' feet; and they distributed to each as anyone had need. [36]And Joses, who was also named Barnabas by the apostles (which is translated Son of Encouragement), a Levite of the country of Cyprus, ³⁷having land, sold *it*, and brought the money and laid *it* at the apostles' feet.

Let me point out a few things you should glean from this passage.

First the Apostles, the preachers, did *not* command them to sell all their possessions. Based upon verses 31 and 32, "And when they had prayed, the place was shaken where they were assembled together; and they were all filled with the Holy Ghost, and they spake the word of God with boldness. And the multitude of them that believed were of one heart and of one soul: neither said any of them that ought of the things which he possessed was his own; but they had all things common." We see the Spirit of God was moving in a powerful way and the **Spirit of God moved upon the people's hearts to give** in this unusual manner.

This wasn't your ordinary commensurable giving, they gave above their means, however verse (33) says, "And with great power gave the apostles witness of the resurrection of the Lord Jesus: and *great grace* was upon them all." The people had **Great Grace** upon them to give on this level.

Note: (You should not attempt to repeat this example of giving unless God has given you Great Grace to do it). We see in verse 34, "Neither was there any among them that lacked: for as many as were possessors of lands or houses sold them, and brought the prices of the things that were sold." This indicates when God is truly behind your giving – no one losses, there's no lack. Notice the Apostles didn't get rich and the members left broke. No, that wasn't the case here.

According to verse 35, "And laid them down at the apostles' feet: and distribution was made unto every man according as he had need." The Apostles had integrity, they distributed according to the people's needs. This was a demonstration of what Paul called church *equality*. Paul says in 2 Corinthians 8:8-15, "I speak not by commandment, but I am testing the sincerity of your love by the diligence of others. For you know the grace of our Lord Jesus Christ, that though He was rich, yet for your sakes He became poor, that you through His poverty might become rich. And in this I give advice: It is to your advantage not only to be doing what you began and were desiring to do a year ago; but now you also must complete the doing *of it*; that as *there was* a readiness to desire *it*, so *there* also *may be* a completion out of what *you* have. For if there is first a willing mind, *it is* accepted according to what one has, *and* not according to what he does not have. *For I do not mean that others should be eased and you burdened; but by an equality, that now at this time your abundance may supply their lack, that their abundance also may supply your lack—**that there may be equality**. As it is written, "He who gathered much had nothing left over; and he who gathered little had no lack."*

In Acts 4, you can see this **principle of equality** being put into practice. People were served according to their needs, henceforth everybody's needs were met. The preachers were not attempting to gain a profit off the peoples giving, nor did they seek self-gain. The truth of the matter is, if the Apostles would've kept the proceeds from this collection, they would have been filthy rich, while the people would have been left broke, busted and disgusted. Had that been the case as we often see today, I guess the people would have had to pray to God to supply their needs supernaturally. What sense would that have made? Unfortunately this happens somewhere every Sunday. People are instructed to tithe regardless of their financial ability and then they are told to believe God to pay those pending bills.

Did the Apostles do that here? No, thank God that didn't occur. The Apostles operated with integrity, they did the right thing and distributed according to the needs of the people. Note: (I'm fully aware that God will ask us to give sacrificially at times to receive a supernatural return, however we should give on that level only when He specifically compels us to).

The lesson to learn is:

1) Give what the Spirit of God has impressed upon your heart.

2) Give according to the grace given to you. Avoid competitive and comparative giving. Competitive and comparative giving is when you strive to match or beat other congregants giving. You're guilty of trying to keep up with the Joneses.

3) If God is directing your giving there will be no lack. If you're giving and there's still lack, first you should evaluate the condition of your heart with giving. What I mean is, you should consider whether or not you're giving reluctantly or from compulsion. Next determine if you're truly operating within integrity and genuinely trying to follow the Spirits leading with giving. I'm reminded of what I heard a pastor once say, "*Because it doesn't look like its working, doesn't mean it isn't working.*" Maybe it's not the season for you to reap the harvest. Galatians 6:9 says, "And let us not be weary in well doing: for in *due season* we shall reap, if we faint not." If your heart is right in your effort to give, God will restore everything you lost plus he'll give you double for your trouble. Reference the story of Job. Job lost everything, yet he endured. Job 42:10 says, "And the Lord restored Job's losses when he prayed for his friends. Indeed the Lord gave Job twice as much as he had before."

Don't stress out over the time you've lost while trusting God. God knows how to catch you up – quoted by Pastor Michael D. Moore.

Let's discuss what happens if you determine you aren't operating in integrity. You realize you've been withholding what God has compelled you to give. Let me answer by telling you when you *know* and fail to give what God has impressed upon your heart, you're not cheating or lying to the preacher or the church, you are cheating God.

Acts 5:1-1, "[1]But a certain man named Ananias, with Sapphira his wife, sold a possession. [2]And he kept back *part* of the proceeds, his wife also being aware *of it*, and brought a certain part and laid *it* at the apostles' feet. [3]<u>But Peter said, "Ananias, why has Satan filled your heart to lie to the Holy Spirit and keep back *part* of the price of the land for yourself?</u> [4]<u>While it remained, was it not your own? And after it was sold, was it not in your own control? Why have you conceived this thing in your heart? You have not lied to men but to God</u>." [5]Then Ananias, hearing these words, fell down and breathed his last. So great fear came upon all those who heard these things. [6]And the young men arose and wrapped him up, carried *him* out, and buried *him*. [7]Now it was about three hours later when his wife came in, not knowing what had happened. [8]And Peter answered her, "Tell me whether you sold the land for so much?" She said, "Yes, for so much." [9]Then Peter said to her, "How is it that you have agreed together to test the Spirit of the Lord? Look, the feet of those who have buried your husband *are* at the door, and they will carry you out." ¹⁰ Then immediately she fell down at his feet and breathed her last. And the young men came in and found her dead, and carrying *her* out, buried *her* by her husband. ¹¹ So great fear came upon all the church and upon all who heard these things.

This passage is a prime example of what happens when we don't operate in integrity of the heart, withholding what the Spirit leads us to give. Here we see a married couple named Ananias and Sapphira. They were given the same Great Grace to give, and leading of the Holy Spirit to give, as the others were given. However, they decided to ignore the Spirits leading and withheld their offering.

> *This is a classic example of New Testament lying and robbing God. It's not withholding the tithes, rather withholding his offering He commanded.*

In verse 3 says, "But Peter said, Ananias, why hath Satan filled thine heart to lie to the Holy Ghost, and to keep back part of the price of the land?" Noticed they weren't accused of lying to the Apostles. They were accused of lying to the Holy Ghost. It's important to note where this lie was conceived. It wasn't conceived when the Apostles confronted them. It was conceived in their **hearts** when they made the decision to disobey. Verse 4 says, "<u>Whiles it remained, was it not thine own? and after it was sold, was it not in thine own power? why hast thou conceived this thing *in thine heart? thou hast not lied unto men, but unto God.*</u>" This is a New Testament case of lying and robbing God. In the Old Testament withholding the tithe was considered robbing God. In the New Testament it is the offering He commands. While we don't have the curse of not tithing in the New Testament, we do have consequences for lying to the Spirit of God in our giving. We see in verse 5, "And Ananias hearing these words fell down, and gave up the ghost: and great fear came on all them that heard these things." They both fell dead as a result of telling this lie to the Holy Spirit. The preachers didn't judge them, the Spirit did. With Great Grace comes either great blessings or great judgement, depending upon the decisions we make to obey or disobey.

> *"Remember give from your heart, but give with integrity believing you're giving what the Spirit of God has impressed upon your heart to give."*

Lastly, in the New Testament all our money and possessions belong to God, we're just stewards over them. A steward understands they don't actually own any of the possessions, they just manage them. To be good stewards we must seek Godly guidance and wisdom to be resourceful with what God has entrusted us with. You will never go wrong if loving people is your objective and motivation.

PRINCIPLE #4: WHEN SHOULD WE GIVE? WHAT SHOULD BE OUR MOTIVATION FOR GIVING?

There are two guiding principles for when we should give:

First, we should give regularly to the *place* where we receive our spiritual food "the Word" and covering.

1 Corinthians 16:1-2

(1) Now concerning the collection for the saints, as I have given <u>orders to the churches of Galatia</u>, even so do ye.

(2) <u>Upon the first day of the week let every one of you lay by him in store</u>, as God hath prospered him, that there be no gatherings when I come.

Paul gave orders to his churches to lay aside an offering on the first day of the week. This suggest we should give regularly to the *place* where we receive our spiritual covering and receive the Word. Notice I said place, and not just your local church. Due to modern day technology we're able to get the Word regularly through multiple mediums.

We can watch or listen to churches all over the world by livestream, television, radio and even subscribe to receive their free spiritual material by mail. If you regularly receive the Word from any of these mediums, you have a biblical responsibility to help support them.

If the material you received made a difference in your life and you in return support them, they can continue producing more material and make a difference in other lives as well.

Romans 15:27 AMP says, "They were pleased to do it; and surely they were in debt to them, for if these Gentiles have come to share in their [Jerusalem Jews] spiritual blessings, then they ought also to be of service to them in material blessings."

Additional reference: 1 Corinthians 9:9-11

Exception to the rule:

(Please be advised this is my spirit-filled opinion. This principle of giving I'm referring to is solely based upon you getting **free** spiritual resources. *When it's free*, it's biblical for you to provide your financial support in return. However, you're *not* obligated to give anything if you've **paid** for the spiritual resources. For instance, if you ***pay*** to attend a Christian conference or concert, you're not obligated to give any offering unless God leads you to do so).

Second, we should give when God shows us a need and then moves upon our heart to meet that need.

Philippians 4:10-19 says, "[10] I rejoiced greatly in the Lord that at last you renewed your concern for me. Indeed, you were concerned, but you <u>had no opportunity to show it</u>. [11] I am not saying this because I am in need, for I have learned to be content whatever the circumstances. [12] I know what it is to be in need, and I know what it is to have plenty. I have learned the secret of being content in any and every situation, whether well fed or hungry, whether living in plenty or in want. [13] I can do all this through him who gives me strength. [14] Yet it was good of you to share in my troubles. [15]*Moreover, as you Philippians know, in the early days of your acquaintance with the gospel, when I set out from Macedonia, not one church shared with me in the matter of giving and receiving, <u>except you only</u>;* [16] for even when I was in Thessalonica, you sent me aid more than once when I was in need. [17] Not that I desire your gifts; what I desire is that more be credited to your account. [18] I have received full payment and have more than enough. I am amply supplied, now that I have received from Epaphroditus the gifts you sent. They are a fragrant offering, an acceptable sacrifice, pleasing to God. [19] And my God will meet all your needs according to the riches of his glory in Christ Jesus.

As stated earlier, the preacher should provide the people the giving opportunity, and then trust the Spirit of God to move upon the peoples' hearts to give accordingly. This is what happened in the passage in verse 10, Paul states, "I rejoiced greatly in the Lord that at last you renewed your concern for me. Indeed, you were concerned, but you <u>*had no opportunity to show it*</u>." We see here the people discovered Paul's need - *the giving opportunity*. Following you see God move upon the people's heart to meet this need verse 18, "I have received full payment and have more than enough. I am amply supplied, now that I have received from Epaphroditus the gifts you sent. They are a fragrant offering, an acceptable sacrifice, pleasing to God."

Do you recall the principle we learned earlier about Spirit-led giving? We learned whenever God is directing us to give to others he has our needs in mind. Paul says in verses 18 & 19, "I have received full payment and have more than enough. I am amply supplied, now that I have received from Epaphroditus the gifts you sent. They are a fragrant offering, an acceptable sacrifice, pleasing to God. [19] And my God will meet all your needs according to the riches of his glory in Christ Jesus." After these people gave as God compelled them to, the promise of God supplying their needs were conferred upon them. Provision is proof-positive that God is behind our giving. [See Reference: 1 Kings 17:8-16]

We're blessed to be a blessing!

PRINCIPLE #5: WHAT SHOULD BE OUR GIVING MOTIVATION?

Our giving motivation should come from a heart of gratitude because we're thankful for what God has done for us. Everyone has a story, the only place you start off on top is digging a hole, and it's downhill thereafter. We should remember where we've come from and what we've been through and give in light of Gods' goodness. You may not be able to repay all the people that helped you along the way, but you can always *pay it forward*. Pay it forward is an old concept which describes a person being the beneficiary of a good deed and rather repaying the benefactor instead you repay it to others.

> *God doesn't need our money in Heaven. Nor does he want us to pay him back. He desires us to pay it forward – bestow goodness on others as he bestowed on us!*

Regardless if you acknowledge God or not, you didn't do it without his help. There were tons of people more educated, talented and prepared, so don't ever become arrogant.

Deuteronomy 8:17-18 says, "Then you say in your heart, my power and the might of my hand have gained me this wealth. And you shall **remember** the Lord your God, for *it is* He who gives you power to get wealth that He may establish His covenant which He swore to your fathers, as *it is* this day."

Freedom and cheerful giving is derived from a heart that remembers what God has done. We freely and generously give because God has freely and generously given us his son. 2 Cor. 8:9 says, "For you know the grace of our Lord Jesus Christ, that though He was rich, yet for your sakes He became poor, that you through His poverty might become rich."

We give freely out of love because God gave to us freely out of love. I've heard this quote frequently at my church, "You can give without loving, but you cannot love without giving." *Our primary motivation for giving should always be rooted in love.* 1 Cor. 13:3 says, "And though I bestow all my goods to feed the poor, and though I give my body to be burned, and have not charity, it profiteth me nothing."

What shouldn't be our giving motivations?

1) Self-gain; Profit (pride)
2) Self-interest (selfishness)
3) Accolades (arrogance)
4) To Get Rich (greed)

PART 3: THE PROSPERITY MESSAGE

1 Timothy 6:5-10 NIV says, "⁵ And constant friction between people of corrupt mind, who have been robbed of

the truth and **who think that godliness is a means to financial gain. ⁶But godliness with contentment is great gain.** ⁷For we brought nothing into the world, and we can take nothing out of it. ⁸ But if we have food and clothing, we will be content with that. ⁹ Those who want to get rich fall into temptation and a trap and into many foolish and harmful desires that plunge people into ruin and destruction. ¹⁰For the love of money is a root of all kinds of evil. Some people, eager for money, have wandered from the faith and pierced themselves with many griefs.

Time to dive into a very controversial subject. There is a message widely known today as the Prosperity Message. This message is largely based upon the premise that God wants us all to be rich. Some who promote this message teach the way to receive is through giving and the greater you give the greater you'll receive in return. I don't object to the law of sowing and reaping. In fact, sowing and reaping is an eternal principle of the earth. Genesis 8:22 says, "While the earth remaineth, seedtime and harvest, and cold and heat, and summer and winter, and day and night shall not cease." Having said that, I don't object to the principle of sowing and reaping. I do fundamentally disapprove of the spirit of the prosperity message some teach. ***"Some" but certainly not all prosperity teachers teach this message as a give-to-get message.*** The Prosperity Message has become so pervasive in some churches today that giving-to-get has been taught as a standard way of getting God to move. Some have portrayed God to be a slot machine, and if you put enough coins in you'll likely hit eventually with a little faith. The state of the church is under attack by secularism. If you don't look like you got it going on as they say, you're likely not be described as blessed. What's more troubling is that if you don't "look" blessed (prosperous), you'll likely not be accept into certain circles within some of today's churches. The church has become pretentious! The bible warns the church against treating people more or less favorable based upon their material possessions.

James 2:1-12 says, "My brethren, do not hold your faith in our glorious Lord Jesus Christ with *an* attitude *of* personal favoritism. For if a man comes into your assembly with a gold ring and dressed in fine clothes, and there also comes in a poor man in dirty clothes, and you pay special attention to the one who is wearing the fine clothes, and say, "You sit here in a good place," and you say to the poor man, "You stand over there, or sit down by my footstool," have you not made distinctions among yourselves, and become judges with evil motives? Listen, my beloved brethren: did not God choose the poor of this world *to be* rich in faith and heirs of the kingdom which He promised to those who love Him? But you have dishonored the poor man. Is it not the rich who oppress you and personally drag you into court? Do they not blaspheme the fair name by which you have been called? If, however, you are fulfilling the royal law according to the Scripture, "YOU

SHALL LOVE YOUR NEIGHBOR AS YOURSELF," you are doing well. But if you show partiality, you are committing sin *and* are convicted by the law as transgressors. 1For whoever keeps the whole law and yet stumbles in one *point*, he has become guilty of all. For He who said, "DO NOT COMMIT ADULTERY," also said, "DO NOT COMMIT MURDER." Now if you do not commit adultery, but do commit murder, you have become a transgressor of the law. So speak and so act as those who are to be judged by *the* law of liberty."

Don't confuse your divine-worth with your net-worth!

The misconception that suggests your external prosperity depicts your true spiritual prosperity is wrong! Believing if you're rich, you're favored of God, while those who are financially challenged aren't is another example of a lie dressed like the truth. This thought-process can't be true because in Genesis 39:21 the bible says Joseph was favored of God, yet his life was full of incredible struggles. Please be advised when you walk with God, it's not uncommon to have dry seasons. Dry seasons are those seasons when nothing seems to be working. You'll even think, where in the world is God? Actually it's through these dry seasons of life God is testing our character. *My pastor once said*, "*God often disguises the promise with a problem.*" Even Jesus was tested, in Matthew 4:1 it states, "Then Jesus was led by the Spirit into the wilderness to be tempted by the devil." *Remember* it's only a test, so don't give up, you'll come out on top when the season ends! James 1:12 says, "Blessed is the man that endureth temptation: for when he is tried, he shall receive the crown of life, which the Lord hath promised to them that love him."

> *External prosperity is no true gauge to determine someone's relationship with God. It's been my observation that all externally rich people aren't honest and smart, and all externally poor people aren't lazy and dumb.*

1 Timothy 6:5-6 says, "And constant friction between people of corrupt mind, who have been robbed of the truth and <u>who think that godliness is a means to financial gain. ⁶But godliness with contentment is great gain</u>. When I read the word *gain* in verse 5, "And constant friction between people of corrupt mind, who have been robbed of the truth and **who think that godliness is a means to financial gain**," I immediately I thought about profit and capitalism. A profit is obtaining a financial advantage or benefit, especially from an investment of something. While capitalism is an economic system in which the means of production and distribution are privately or corporately owned and the operations are funded by profits. Paul strongly warns the church not to operate as a capitalistic organization. Paul says in verse 6, "But godliness with contentment is great gain." Paul's point is godliness is not about gain, so we shouldn't be driven by a profit mentality. How unfortunate it is that this mindset has seeped into the church.

Nowadays inside most churches almost nothing is free, everything has a price connected to it.

This capitalist mind-set comes from the world's mentality - secularism. In our Western society much of our anxiety and lack of contentment has absolutely nothing to do with God not being a good provider, especially to America. It's about our voracious appetite for more, more, and more. In America today we have an unbridled lust and greed for the next best and bigger thing. This secular spirit of greed has seeped into some of our churches. This spirit of greed was very subtle. It entered under the pretext God wanted his children rich, which is what some prosperity messages have conveyed.

If you take a moment and think about it, doesn't that theme sound like a lottery or casino advertisement? The ad, "Come play today and take a chance to hit it big, at the "Lawd Help Me Now Casino," the place where the more you give the more chances you have to win big and get rich! A little funny, huh? Sad, but it's terribly true.

Some of these messages of prosperity have created immense problems for some people to trust the church's motive for collecting money. This message has also negatively affected some Christians' giving motives. They should be giving from the heart as the Spirit-leads or commensurable to their prosperity. Now most Christians give from selfish motivations and often above their ability in an effort to gain. James 4:2-3 AMP says, "You are jealous and covet [what others have] and your lust goes unfulfilled; so you murder. You are envious and cannot obtain [the object of your envy]; so you fight and battle. <u>You do not have because you do not ask [it of God]. You ask [God for something] and do not receive it, because you ask with wrong motives [out of selfishness or with an unrighteous agenda], so that [when you get what you want] you may spend it on your [hedonistic] desires.</u>"

God isn't going to ignore our hearts' motives when we give. You can give as much as you like, however he's not going to bless our selfish agendas. No wonder some of today's believers aren't seeing much or any results at all. Because they're giving from the wrong motive. Not taking any shots at any particular preachers, but it's obvious they're church is going to prosper from this giving regardless if it's spirit-directed or frivolous donations. In case you didn't know, the church is a BUSINESS. Once again, this isn't a shot at any church in particular. This a shot at the prosperity teachers who communicate directly or indirectly that godliness is about gain. Please know great churches with amazing leaders do exist.

Question: What are your motives for giving?

In 1 Timothy 6:9, Paul sharply warns Christians to beware of the get rich mentality. To add emphasis to this point, I've provided this verse in four different translations.

1 Timothy 6:9 (NIV) - Those who **want to get rich** fall into temptation and a trap and into many foolish and harmful desires that plunge people into ruin and destruction."

1 Timothy 6:9 (NKJV) - But those who **desire to be rich** fall into temptation and a snare, and *into* many foolish and harmful lusts which drown men in destruction and perdition."

1 Timothy 6:9 (AMP) - But those who [are not financially ethical and] **crave to get rich** [with a compulsive, greedy longing for wealth] fall into temptation and a trap and into many foolish and harmful desires that plunge people into ruin and destruction [leading to personal misery].

1 Timothy 6:9 (KJV) - But they that **will be rich** fall into temptation and a snare, and into many foolish and hurtful lusts, which drown men in destruction and perdition.

Highlight the words *want, desire, crave and will*. Paul said those (Christians) that *want, desire, crave and will* themselves to be rich evitable will fall. Yes, when your motivation is all about getting rich you open the door for Satan to come in with his "wicked suggestions". Most of his wicked suggestions will seem like "Godly ideals", however they're actually traps that lead to ruin and destruction. 2 Corinthians 11:14-15 says, "For such men are false apostles, deceitful workers, masquerading as apostles of Christ. And no wonder, for Satan himself masquerades as an angel of light. It is not surprising, then, if his servants masquerade as servants of righteousness. Their end will correspond to their actions." Do not be deceived, believers particularly church leaders focus their "wills" on getting rich, they oftentimes wind up in some form of CORRUPTION.

Is corruption really in the church? Yes, and it's not unusual for corruption to be in the church. Actually, Jesus had to address it during his earthly ministry. Matthew 21:12-13, "And Jesus went into the temple of God, and cast out all them that sold and bought in the temple, and overthrew the tables of the moneychangers, and the seats of them that sold doves, And said unto them, It is written, My house shall be called the house of prayer; but ye have made it a den of thieves."

Corruption both inside and outside the church always stems from the love of money. 1 Timothy 6:10 says, "For the love of money is the root of all evil: which while some coveted after, they have erred from the faith, and pierced themselves through with many sorrows." Many times we use this scripture in reference to unsaved worldly people who chase money. Please be advised, this wasn't directed to them. Although it does apply, it was addressed to church folk. Yes, the lovers of money scripture was addressed to the church, not the world! Allow me to prove this. The first part of that verse says, "For the love of money is the root of all evil: which while some coveted after." The second part says, "<u>They have erred from the faith</u>, and pierced themselves through with many sorrows." Notice it says, "***They have erred from the FAITH.***" The word "*they*" refers to believers and the phrase "*the faith*" refers to Christianity.

I remember when the prosperity message movement first began. I'd just given my life to Christ. The message initially was healthy and sincere. It was about biblical economics and stewardship. Overtime it's been polluted by some preachers that began making godliness about gain, most became corrupted by the love of money. The give-to-get message, *prosperity message*, has become a multi-million dollar business strategy for "some" churches. It's no surprise why the teaching of tithing has so been heavily promoted by some churches. *No one ever cares about what's right when something is working.* I'm here saying the message of giving has been distorted! Due to this distortion some non-believers won't step a foot inside the church today. Also, there are some believers who have been offended because of the emphasis placed on money, and they've discontinued going regularly to church.

People see some preachers dressing, driving, and flying in things only the super-rich can afford, while the average church member is likely struggling to make ends meet. Seeing these preachers live this super extravagant lifestyle has caused many to speculate their true motives. Let me be perfectly clear, all successful pastors aren't crooks. Some are doing things the right way and are simply blessed as a result. Proverbs 10:22 says, "The blessing of the Lord makes *one* rich, and He adds no sorrow with it."

Jesus says in Mark 12:38-40, "And he said unto them in his doctrine, Beware of the scribes, which love to go in long clothing, and love salutations in the marketplaces, and the chief seats in the synagogues, and the uppermost rooms at feasts: Which devour widows' houses, and for a pretense make long prayers: these shall receive greater damnation." I'm am not saying a preacher shouldn't live a blessed lifestyle. The word *blessed* is subjective, it's based upon one's own ideal. However whenever we do things as believers we must consider the impact on our fellow brothers and sisters. This is especially true for church leaders. Church leaders should really consider the potential impact on others before they do and say certain things. Some things aren't sins, they are just unwise and unproductive decisions. Paul says 1 Corinthians 8:10-13 says, " For if anyone sees you who have knowledge eating in an idol's temple, will not the conscience of him who is weak be emboldened to eat those things offered to idols? And because of your knowledge shall the weak brother perish, for whom Christ died? But when you thus sin against the brethren, and wound their weak conscience, you sin against Christ. Therefore, if food makes my brother stumble, I will never again eat meat, lest I make my brother stumble."

Paul further emphasized this point in 1 Corinthians 10:23-24, he states, "All things are lawful for me, but not all things are helpful; all things are lawful for me, but not all things edify. Let no one seek his own, but each one the other's *well-being.*"

I am not against leaders living luxurious lifestyles, however I am saying that if something we're doing is causing a massive amount of people to stumble and be offended with God that becomes an act of *selfishness*. I'm sure you've witnessed some preachers drive a hundred thousand dollar vehicle through the church parking lot where their average member can barely afford a vehicle. That's not the example Jesus displayed during his earthly ministry. Jesus made himself of no reputation! Philippians 2:7 says, "But made himself of no reputation, and took upon him the form of a servant, and was made in the likeness of men."

> *"Whoever wants to become great among you must be your servant"* - Matthew 20:26$_b$

Even Paul was so passionate about the message of Christ and his love for the church he often made financial sacrifices to avoid his motives from being questioned. We should consider Paul's example and compare to what we see modeled in some of our churches today. Paul states in 2 Corinthians 8:16-21, "But thanks be to God who puts the same genuine concern for you in the heart of Titus. For Titus not only accepted our appeal, but was so very interested in you that he has gone to visit you of his own accord. And we have sent along with him the brother who is praised in the gospel [ministry] throughout all the churches; and not only this, but he has also been appointed by the churches to travel with us in regard to this *gracious offering* which we are administering for the glory of the Lord Himself, and to show our eagerness [as believers to help one another]. <u>We are taking precaution so that no one will [find anything with which to] discredit us in our administration of this generous gift. For we have regard for what is honorable [and above suspicion], not only in the sight of the Lord, but also in the sight of men.</u>"

One translation describes this offering as being a very large offering. While Paul was appreciative of the offering, he wanted to ensure it was handled with integrity and wisdom. I say integrity and wisdom because of what Paul said, "For we have regard for what is honorable [and above suspicion], not only in the *<u>sight of the Lord</u>*, but *<u>also in the sight of men</u>*."

It's an act of integrity when we live honorable lives **in the *sight of God in private*.** Also, it's wisdom to understand we must **appear** honorable in ***the sight of man in public***. (Maybe if the church had more financial transparency, there would be less suspicion and false accusation assigned to its prosperity).

In order to avoid being under the cloud of suspicion which would hinder the gospel, Paul often worked. Paul states in Acts 20:33-35, "I have coveted no man's silver, or gold, or apparel. Yea, ye yourselves know, that these hands have ministered unto my necessities, and to them that were with me. I have shewed you all things, how that so labouring ye ought to support the weak, and to remember the words of the Lord Jesus, how he said, It is more blessed to give than to receive."

Paul simply did not practice or teach the prosperity message we often hear today being taught. Granted, Paul had every right to take compensation for his service. Oftentimes he chose to use his craft as a tentmaker to generate a stream of income, so he wouldn't be a financial burden to the people he served. Acts 18:1-3 "After this Paul left Athens and went to Corinth. There he met a Jew named Aquila, a native of Pontus, who had recently come from Italy with his wife, Priscilla, because [the Roman Emperor] Claudius had issued an edict that all the Jews were to leave Rome. Paul went to see them, and because he was of the same trade, he stayed with them; and they worked together for they were tent-makers." 2 Thessalonians 3:7-9 "For you yourselves know how you ought to follow us, for we were not disorderly among you; **nor did we eat anyone's bread free of charge, but worked with labor and toil night and day, that we might not be a burden to any of you, not because we do not have authority, but to make ourselves an example of how you should follow us.**"

That's why it's critical we not only *pray **for*** our leaders, but we should also *pray **about*** our leaders as well. We should endeavor to have a leader who has the humility of Jesus.

Philippians 2:3-9 says, "Do nothing out of selfish ambition or vain conceit. Rather, in humility value others above yourselves, not looking to your own interests but each of you to the interests of the others. In your relationships with one another, have the same mindset as Christ Jesus: Who, being in very nature of God, did not consider equality with God something to be used to his own advantage; rather, he made himself nothing by taking the very nature of a servant, being made in human likeness. And being found in appearance as a man, he humbled himself by becoming obedient to death – even death on a cross! *Therefore God has exalted him to the highest place and gave him the name that is above every name.*" You do understand Jesus could have come down to earth in all his Heavenly majesty and power and reigned, but he didn't. Mainly because that would have hindered his earthly purpose. Jesus loved us so much, he stripped himself of all Heavenly entitlements, and came to earth to ultimately die in shame and agony for you and me to be saved. Amazing! Jesus knew who he was. Earthly material things didn't make him more or less than a king, he exhibited true humility. Humility isn't to be mistaken for thinking less of ourselves, rather it's thinking of ourselves less. Jesus' example of humility demonstrates we shouldn't seek to gain earthly riches and recognition, rather we should eagerly seek God's purpose and He'll not only bless our lives, he will also give us a name.

Humility isn't thinking less of yourself, rather thinking of yourself less – Rick Warren

Here's a few suggestions for what you should be asking God about your leader. Ask God does your leader love you or the dollars you represent when you join their church? Ask God is your leader genuinely hungry for souls or just a big church? Ask God does your leader desire to be on television to have a world renowned ministry to be a hot-shot preacher? Today there are many God-fearing leaders in the body of Christ, however there are some fake ones as well disguised as the real thing. Which one is leading you – the real or fake one? You should know, 1 Thessalonians 5:1 says, "And we beseech you, brethren, to know them which labour among you, and are over you in the Lord, and admonish you." It's not a sin to measure your leader by God's Words – the Word clearly outlines the standard(s) for church leadership. Henceforth, stop making excuses for church leaders' poor behavior. Be mindful if God allows you to see something, it may be for your good and others. Don't be intimidated or afraid to call it like you see it – call a spade a spade!

Now Paul exemplified true love for the church in action and in deeds. Notice what he says in 1 Thessalonians 2:8-9, "So we cared for you. Because we loved you so much, we were delighted to share with you not only the gospel of God but our lives as well. Surely you remember, brothers and sisters, our toil and hardship; **we worked night and day in order not to be a burden to anyone while we preached the gospel of God to you.**"

The point here is that Paul had a heart for reaching souls and he wouldn't allow the cloud of suspicion related to money hinder his message, so he operated in his gift without charge. Paul (served) preached the gospel FREE without any strings attached. People operating in their gifts for free, don't happen a lot nowadays. Most highly gifted and skilled people in the body of Christ oftentimes won't serve (use their gift or skill) unless they're getting paid. Never think the most gifted or skilled people serving are the ones *standing*. Oftentimes it's the ones *sitting*.

Hopefully, I've proven to you that pure New Testament giving is simply a byproduct of love. To keep our giving and service to God pure, we should periodically evaluate our motives. Below I've listed some indicators and red flags that will indicate your giving motives may be off.

Red Flags to indicate your giving motives may be off:

1) Internal jealousy and frustration because nothing is working. You've done the 21-steps to a breakthrough numerous of times and you're still in a mess.
2) You're offended with the church and God. You've become cynical of others prosperity.
3) Lottery mentality: You find yourself giving more and more hoping you hit the big jackpot.

Nevertheless, if you're giving is purposeful and/or Spirit-led according to 2 Corinthians 9:8-10 you'll inevitably see these results. It says, "And God *is* able to make all grace abound toward you, that you, always having all sufficiency in all *things*, may have an abundance for every good work. As it is written: "He has dispersed abroad, He has given to the poor; His righteousness endures forever." Now may He who supplies seed to the sower, and bread for food, supply and multiply the seed you have *sown* and increase the fruits of your righteousness." [2 Corinthians 9:8-10]

God promised to:

1) Give you favor so you won't need any aid or support

2) Open supernatural doors – *External Prosperity.*

3) Supply you with more seed to sow

4) Multiply your seed sown

5) Bless you with internal righteousness that will manifest itself in peace of mind, contentment, joy and satisfaction – *Internal Prosperity*

Spirit-led giving is the New Testament giving that brings glory to God.

Noticed what it states in 2 Corinthians 9:11-13, "You will be enriched in every way so that you can be generous on every occasion, and through us your generosity will result in thanksgiving to God. This service that you perform is not only supplying the needs of the Lord's people but is also overflowing in many expressions of thanks to God. *Because of the service by which you have proved yourselves, others will praise God for the obedience that accompanies your confession of the gospel of Christ, and for your generosity in sharing with them and with everyone else.*

When we follow the Spirit of God leading in our giving, people are helped, our needs are met and God is ultimately glorified.

I unashamedly don't tithe, I give! Prior to receiving this understanding from the Spirit of God, I spent years feeling ashamed and condemned when I missed tithing. Since I was taught I was robbing God if I didn't tithe, I felt like I was disappointing God. I was led to believe I was living under a closed heaven, cursed with a curse. I truly loved the Lord, however I didn't think I could afford to give the church ten percent every time I got paid.

For years I believed God was angry with me. As I said before this belief led me to dodge God in my conscience. Dodging God in my conscience led to a lack of confidence in my prayer life, and ultimately shying away from the church for years. 1 John 5:14-15 says, "And this is the confidence that we have in him, that, if we ask any thing according to his will, he heareth us: And if we know that he hear us, whatsoever we ask, we know that we have the petitions that we desired of him." The enemy knows confidence is critical to your prayer life, without prayer you lack the power to fight off the enemy, you'll likely live as a defeated Christian as I did. James 5:16 AMP says, "Therefore, confess your sins to one another [your false steps, your offenses], and pray for one another, that you may be healed *and* restored. *The heartfelt and persistent prayer of a righteous man (believer) can accomplish much [when put into action and made effective by God—it is dynamic and can have tremendous power].*"

I thought I was a thief because I was allegedly stealing God's money - the tithe. I honestly thought I owed God money. After getting this revelation concerning tithing, I realized I didn't owe God, and I wasn't a thief. Immediately I was set completely free! This freedom is what inspired me to write this book to help others, who maybe struggling like I was. I desperately want you to realize Gods love for you isn't based upon the size of your offering, rather the size of your heart giving it. It makes perfect sense! Imagine if your kid wanted to surprise you for your birthday, so they made you a birthday card in school. On your birthday they wake you up out of your sleep excited to hand you this handmade card. I'm sure you wouldn't see the card, and ask, "Is this all I'm getting for my birthday?" Of course not, you'll gladly accept it because it's not the size of the gift that matters, it's the size of their heart giving it. You know if they could have done better they would have. How much more does God understand our willingness versus our ability? 1 Corinthians 8:12 says, "For if there is first a willing mind, *it is* accepted according to what one has, *and* not according to what he does not have."

Remember God isn't concerned with the size of your gift, it's the size of your heart giving it that matters!

Mark 12:41-44 says, "Jesus sat down opposite the place where the offerings were put and watched the crowd putting their money into the temple treasury. **Many rich people threw in large amounts. But a poor widow came and put in two very small copper coins, worth only a few cents.** Calling his disciples to him, Jesus said, "Truly I tell you, **this poor widow has put more into the treasury than all the others.** They all gave out of their wealth; but she, out of her poverty, put in everything—all she had to live on."

Jesus said the widow woman gave **MORE** than the rich guys. It wasn't more in terms of the actual amount size. It was more because of the size of her heart. While the rich guys gave from their large bank accounts, the poor widow gave the very little she had. However she gave the little she had from the heart, that's why her gift was so significant.

> *Always remember, "Worldly success doesn't mean Godly significance!"*

In conclusion of this study I want to encourage you to begin realizing God loves you regardless of your seemingly insignificant contribution. Your gift may be insignificant to man, but it's great to God. Remember God sees your heart when you give. He knows our real financial story, the one we hide from family, friends and church folk.

I encourage you to release all those negative feelings related to not tithing and begin today giving the New Testament way!

Hey, if you were to die today, where would you spend eternity? God loves you so much, he gave his only son, so you can have a right to spend eternity in Heaven. The bible says there are only two places to spend eternity - heaven or hell. If you don't believe they exist, that doesn't make it less of a reality. The question is, do you want to gamble on your eternal destination? Have you ever been wrong before? If so, maybe this is another instance. If you'd like to give your heart to Christ, please confess this simple prayer.

Dear God, I want to be a part of your family. I repent of my sins, I acknowledge that Jesus died for my sins and I accept Him as my Lord and Savior. God you said if I call upon the name Jesus, I would be saved. So God, I now say that I believe Jesus died for me, I believe you raised him from the dead for me and that He is alive and well. I accept Him now as my personal Lord and Savior. I accept my salvation from sin right now. I believe I am now saved. Jesus is my Lord. Jesus is my Savior. Thank you, Father God, for forgiving me, saving me, and giving me eternal life. Amen! Congratulations you're now a born-again Christian!

If this book has made a difference in your life, I'd love to hear from you!

Write or email me:

Johnny L Sharp
P O Box 81192
Atlanta, GA 30366

jsharplegacy@gmail.com

Coming soon!!

Volume 2: The Naked Truth about Racism in the Church

Made in the USA
Columbia, SC
06 July 2022